THE CHEMISTRY TATTOO

Solving the Science of Lasting Relationships

by Mae Chinn Songer, MS, LMHC
Edited by Sheryl R. Grassie, Ed.D.

Comfort PUBLISHING

THE CHEMISTRY TATTOO

For information, address Comfort Publishing, 296 Church St. N., Concord, NC 28025. The views expressed in this book are not necessarily those of the publisher.

First printing

Book cover design
by Reed Karriker

ISBN: 978-1-938388-32-3
Published by Comfort Publishing, LLC
www.comfortpublishing.com

Printed in the United States of America

Table of Contents

ACKNOWLEDGEMENT

There are two women to whom I owe an enormous debt of gratitude. My Agent, Laurie Harper, who not only persisted until she found a publisher for my work, but she led me to my editor, Dr. Sheryl Grassie who literally taught me to write, and helped me birth this book. It would not have happened without either of them. Thank you, Laurie and Sheryl, from the bottom of my heart. Both Laurie Harper, owner of Author Biz Consulting and Dr. Sheryl Grassie, Executive Director of End of the Spectrum, a non-profit for autism, are from Minneapolis, MN.

Introduction

Why the Chemistry Tattoo

"The quality of your life is the quality of your relationships."
— *Anthony Robbins*

In the course of deciding to write this book — a book about creating successful long-term relationships — I have pondered numerous metaphors to describe its content. I originally conceptualized it as an awakening process, a progressive awareness of who we really are that allows us to connect with others in a more meaningful way.

Awareness enables us to discover ourselves at a deeper level, away from the "false self" many of us have created to function in the world. When we really understand who we are, and what we believe, we can clearly see the foundation from which we have chosen the people in our lives. We can clearly see the beliefs that underlie our connections to others.

You may be one of the lucky ones who can say without hesitation that you truly know yourself, but the majority of us cannot. Honestly and intimately knowing ourselves, and understanding our belief systems, is a prerequisite for the work of creating successful and lasting relationships. What we believe about ourselves and others is operating underneath our feelings and actions, and an awareness of those beliefs allows us to see what our relationship foundations are.

Although awareness of our beliefs is a key, the questions arise: How do we become aware? Why aren't we aware now? And, if we are not aware, if we are unconscious of our beliefs, how specifically are they affecting our relationships? As I got into the meat of this book, I realized a more appropriate metaphor would incorporate an understanding that something unconscious is really at the root of our relationship decisions. Unconscious beliefs are driving each of us to choose our friends and especially our partners. Something unconscious is sustaining our patterns in relationships.

The Question

As a therapist, I find myself routinely asking couples in my practice to explain why they chose each other over all the people they could have chosen. The most frequent response I get is, "I don't know how to explain it, it was just chemistry." We all experience this chemistry as a kind of inexplicable attraction, a driving force that motivates us to connect with certain people and choose certain partners. In reflecting on this chemistry — this attraction that acts as the antecedent for most personal relationships — I decided to focus this material on explaining how that chemistry, that driving force, works. Where exactly does it come from, and why does it appear to be permanently etched or tattooed into our consciousness?

The question I set out to answer in his book is, "What underlies the chemical attraction we have towards others and how does it impact our relationships?" This includes friends and lovers, co-workers and family members. My professional career has been dedicated to helping people work through the obstacles that inhibit the success of their relationships. Essentially, I help people understand how to choose wisely, and once chosen, how to keep their relationships happy and enduring.

The Answer

Consistently, what gets in the way of successful relationships is unconscious thinking. Thinking that has been imprinted or tattooed into our brain chemistry, creating limiting beliefs. Tattooed or imprinted beliefs can act as unconscious roadblocks and they can, and often do, generate a feeling of what I call "conditioned chemistry."

This conditioned chemistry is the unconscious attraction we all feel towards certain people. It is the unconscious motivator that directs us to connect with one person over another. Whether in romantic relationships, social connections or in the workplace, we choose the people in our lives based on attraction, and that attraction is predicated on our conditioned chemistry. This book is primarily about understanding and changing your tattooed chemistry; thus the metaphor: *The Chemistry Tattoo.*

Everyone's tattooed chemistry is based on limited or erroneous beliefs to one degree or another. How, then, do we trust the chemistry we feel? How do we trust the feelings of attraction that we have for another person? How do we know that what we feel will take us into a good relationship, and how do we make a good relationship last once we find one?

The answer to these questions is both simple and complicated. Simple, in that successful relationships are almost completely based on healthy beliefs about relationships; complicated, in that we must understand and change our unhealthy, often unconscious, beliefs about relationships in order to have success.

How it Works in Relationships

In more than 25 years of clinical practice, I have come to realize that although most of us are not aware of it, we handpick the people in our lives to be exactly the way they are because it reinforces what we unconsciously expect. In reality, our core beliefs play a central role in those we pick as friends, and colleagues, and partners. For example, if I hold a core belief (usually unconscious) that says, "I am unlovable," I will choose a partner who is cold, or critical, or unsupportive. I will consequently feel unloved, thereby reinforcing my belief.

When a client says to me, "He makes me feel," I tell her that no one can make us feel what we don't already believe. These beliefs are tattooed into our subconscious, out of our awareness, and they motivate us to feel chemistry with certain people. Our beliefs are tattooed into a kind of conditioned chemistry that can sabotage our ability to make positive relationship choices.

Year after year in my practice, I see this hold true. Regardless of the therapy model I have used with a client — be it interpersonal, cognitive or psychodynamic therapy — it all comes down to the same basic problem: limiting conditioned beliefs underlie the feelings of chemistry that interfere with finding and sustaining positive relationships.

Core Beliefs

So what, really, are our unconscious core beliefs? How do these unconscious belief patterns result in a particular attraction or feeling of chemistry towards another person? How is chemistry created?

Core beliefs and the way we behave because of them originated early in our development and are based on how we each responded to our environment as young children. We came into this world with inherited traits and our environment either reinforced or diminished them, but either way, the combination of our genetics and our environment resulted in a set of understandings or beliefs about ourselves, about our relationships and about the world in which each of us operates.

As children we start forming these beliefs long before we develop verbal ability. We decide how best to survive based on how we are treated and what is going on around us. We develop behavior patterns based on the experiences we had, primarily with the powerful people in our lives, usually our parents. These survival patterns translate into specific beliefs that live in our unconscious and we use them to relate to the larger world.

There is now compelling neuroscience indicating that these

early life experiences literally become part of the chemical functioning of our brains. Dr. Jack Shonoff, a Harvard University professor, wrote about this in his book: Neurons to Neighborhoods. He writes about neuron communities in our brains containing deeply etched neural pathways that maintain beliefs and behaviors that either nourish or sabotage our success.

We have all heard stories about children who made positive decisions to become successful, to be doctors, engineers, lawyers or achieve notoriety in some form, and then they did. It is also true that children make decisions and form neural pathways that lead them into unfulfilling, sometimes even failed or self-destructive, relationships and lives.

As children we adapt to our environment and make the best choices we can. The development of our limiting core beliefs was at first a positive and proactive response to the world around us. With simple understandings, and no control over our surroundings, we made the best decisions we were capable of making about ourselves, others and the way relationships should be. These decisions were then etched into our brain chemistry, creating specific neural pathways, and eventually neuron communities, that program us to fulfill certain beliefs.

Now, just as the clothes that fit us as children don't fit us as adults, some of the understandings we formed as children don't work well for us as grown-ups, and in fact, can prevent successful relationships.

In Summary

It is my goal to help anyone who wants to have successful relationships to do so. Although some of the concepts in this book are not new, what is new is that I have developed methods to permanently change unhealthy beliefs that will subsequently change the unhealthy part of your chemical attraction.

Just as I do for the clients in my practice, in this book I put principles into action to give you, my reader, tools for transformation. By the simple act of reading *The Chemistry Tattoo,* you will gain a more comprehensive understanding of your relationships, what limits them and how they can be more successful.

The principles and practices outlined in the following chapters will help you alter your chemical attraction to the "wrong" partners, and help you alter unhealthy patterns in your current relationships. It is my hope and belief that this book will help you find and sustain satisfying, long-lasting relationships.

Chapter One

About Changing Chemistry

*"We can't solve problems by using the same kind of thinking
we used when we created them."*
— *Albert Einstein*

My own life has led me to a firsthand experience of what can happen in your life and relationships when you change your chemistry. Perhaps one reason I have been so successful in supporting my clients is that I had a personal experience of the work I now do and how profound it can be. Before I get into specifics about the concepts and techniques, I'd like to share with you a little of my own personal story.

I came out of a childhood that was riddled with abuse and deprivation. I left home at a young age and made my way in the world, but I was never really successful with my close relationships. As a young adult I felt fortunate to have escaped that environment. What I didn't realize was that I had not escaped the monkeys that came along on my back as I ran away and how they would impact my relationships in the future.

By the time I was in my early 30s, I was feeling extremely agitated and my discomfort was reaching a level that I could not endure. Single and lonely, I was having trouble creating a satisfying, long-lasting relationship. My knowledge about love and connection was proving ineffective and I couldn't seem to stay partnered. I was stuck and desperately wanted change. My un-partnered status was a daily confront, causing me a great deal of pain. I had no way to understand what was happening, and no way to understand the anxiety and depression that were plaguing me. I just knew that too many of my days were filled with loneliness and fear and I could no longer continue with the way things were. My energy for life was waning, which was completely unlike me. I knew I needed to find answers.

Early on, I had developed a pattern for managing my life that allowed me to function fairly well. If I wanted something — whether a job or a relationship — I worked as hard as I possibly could to get it. I gave it everything I had, and generally that strategy proved successful. However, if that approach didn't work, if the job or relationship didn't pan out, I quit, pure and simple. I left the job or terminated the relationship and moved on to something else. Sometimes my leaving was abrupt and other times it would take months or years, but once I left, it was done and I didn't look back.

At this point in my early 30s, however, moving on was proving to be a nearly impossible option. I was stuck and I couldn't bring myself to leave. I was in love with a brilliant and multi-talented man, and in spite of the fact that the relationship wasn't working, my desire to stay was as strong as my desire to leave.

The chemistry I felt for this person was undeniable, but the relationship wasn't viable. I was in a quandary because he was, quite literally, "the man of my dreams" and I couldn't imagine giving him up. I couldn't break the chemical hold he had on me and I couldn't make the relationship work. There were a number of complicated issues, but the bottom line was that he just couldn't commit. At age 33, I had never been married and I knew what I wanted. I wanted to settle down with this man I loved. So, as this was not proving an option, I was struggling once again with the desire to bail, to run.

Up until this point, much of my life had been a classic rags to riches story: the quintessential American dream come true, where, with perseverance, I had been able to overcome that childhood of deprivation and become "successful." I ran away from a severely dysfunctional home when I was just 13, and I worked diligently to follow the promise of the American Dream. I got an education, pursued a career in business and worked relentlessly so that everything would be okay. I put myself through college, found lucrative employment, bought the house, the car, the dog, but something was always missing.

Finally, the awareness that I couldn't continue as before fully dawned. I realized that I had been lonely since the day I left home and the only solution was to create a long-lasting, intimate connection with someone. Even after all my material success, I was constantly hungering for something more. My riches were not bringing me peace and happiness, and I was agitated, feeling restless and lacking purpose. I wanted connection and I wanted commitment.

In contrast to the success of my work and financial life, my personal relationships had always been tricky. Romantic relationships, in particular, had been difficult for me and I couldn't really understand why. I was constantly attracted to the wrong men. This conundrum kept me focused on work and I excelled there.

In my family I had been a "Daddy's girl," the favorite, and I had certain expectations about how I should be treated. Working relationships with men were fine, but the chemistry I experienced with men in romantic relationships was never right. The ones I really wanted didn't want me and the ones that really wanted me, I didn't want. I received several offers of marriage, but none were the man I was looking for. I wanted something I couldn't have.

From the day I left home as a 13-year-old, I had lived without the deep connection I needed and I believed a committed relationship would give me that connection, that fulfillment. But, given that I couldn't seem to create it, and that I was repeatedly chemically attracted to men I couldn't have, I was totally at odds with how to make my intimate relationships with men work.

Therapy

One stormy morning, after a long and sleepless night, I picked up the phone and called a therapist. This was not an easy thing for me to do, but I had to find solutions. I came from the coal mining hills of Kentucky where folks had always believed therapists were for "crazy" people, but I was desperate. So I dialed the number a friend had given me and jumped off the cliff.

That phone call, and the therapy sessions that followed, marked a literal turning point in my life. I was eager to learn a different way — one that would bring me relief — and I was lucky enough to have found someone who could guide me through that process. It was not an easy task.

At that point in my life, although I was a good student and eager to change, I lacked trust and was extremely non-compliant about certain issues. The things I had going for me were that I truly loved learning, and I was miserable enough that I had to have relief. My therapist structured the sessions as a learning experience, which helped engage me. His method — once he had helped me define the problem — was to start at the beginning and examine my relationships with men. This, of course, meant understanding my connection with my father and how that was the foundation for all my subsequent liaisons with men.

What I learned during therapy was that my problems with men, and whom I was attracted to, were the result of early conditioning. This early conditioning resulted in a conditioned chemistry that determined the type of man I would become attracted to. I had made decisions and formed beliefs in my early childhood that were still directing how I thought, who I liked and didn't like, and the kind of involvements I kept having as an adult.

Although some of my beliefs were positive regarding my abilities — hence my career success — many of my beliefs were problematic regarding relationships. My early decisions may have worked well when I was a child, but they were seriously interfering with my ability to function in interpersonal relationships now that I had matured.

These childhood decisions had long since left my awareness but they remained tattooed in my unconscious, directing my thoughts and actions, directing the chemistry I felt for others. They were still, many decades later, dictating and controlling whom I was attracted to and what kind of relationships I created. Those childhood patterns were running the show, acting as troublemakers without my even knowing it.

But it was time to get to know them, time to step back from the constant striving to succeed and consciously decide what was going to run the show in my personal life. It was time to be in the driver's seat and take charge of how my relationships were going to be. It was time to understand why I was in love with a man that couldn't commit.

During my early years in therapy, I worked hard to understand what beliefs were underlying my current decisions. I came to better understand myself, my family and my relationships. I learned how common it is for people to stop themselves from getting what they want, and I learned how to change that. I learned how to remove the chemical tattoos. I was able to alter those early thought patterns, tame those core beliefs that had become troublemakers and turn my relationships around. Oh, and by the way, I did marry that man of my dreams and we are still happy after 35 years of marriage.

From Therapy to Therapist

It was because of my experience in therapy that I came to realize that I, too, wanted to be a therapist. I wanted to help people find their way to successful relationships and, thus, a happier life. After working on automatic pilot in the business world for years, I realized that understanding and working with relationships, and what directs peoples' lives, was my calling. I wanted to commit my life to learning about human behavior.

With this realization, I returned to school to pursue a graduate degree in psychology and become a clinician. I have now been helping people find more meaningful connections, and create new and more productive partnerships for more than 25 years. It was through my own therapeutic experience, my training and education in various psychotherapy models, and my work with thousands of clients that I have developed and refined a therapeutic process that consistently results in positive change.

I am passionate about this process and what it can offer. I have seen it literally transform people's relationships, save marriages from the brink of divorce, help people deepen their existing connections, or find and choose appropriate partners. This work is what motivates me to get up in the morning and what carries me throughout the day.

Core Beliefs

My personal transformation has been an ongoing process. Over the years, as I worked on my own issues and those of my clients, I came to realize that people aren't finding appropriate partners or keeping long-term relationships for one very fundamental reason. They are all operating from belief systems: the conditioned chemistry formed in their early childhood that sabotages their success.

Most adults are too driven by their unconscious beliefs to comprehend why their relationships are not working. Let's face it, most people never think about their unconscious beliefs, period. So the choices we make in attempting to change what isn't working are similar to the blind walking around without their guide dog. Like them, we are moving uncertainly in the dark.

As I have continued with my own therapy and my private practice as a psychotherapist, I have become more and more convinced that we can find happiness and success in relationships by changing our belief systems. Beliefs can limit our success and happiness, or guarantee it, depending on what they are. My work in therapy helped me realize that, as a small child, living in poverty, neglect and violence, I had decided, "I'm all alone, and it's all up to me." These beliefs were primarily responsible for how I lived my life, how hard I worked and why I believed I had to do it all by myself.

These core beliefs, and the resulting conditioned chemistry, were also responsible for the difficulties I experienced in romantic relationships. My belief was that I was all alone, so how could I connect to someone who would commit to me and disprove my belief; my unconscious wouldn't let me. It directed me to people who ensured I stay alone. To change these challenges, I needed to change my core beliefs.

All children develop both positive and negative attitudes about themselves and compelling beliefs about how their relationships will be. These beliefs develop early in life and are unconsciously maintained. Then, as adults, we continue to operate from these childhood understandings, which don't necessarily work in creating satisfying adult relationships. We must uncover and face these beliefs or continue a life we don't really want. Without conscious intervention, these beliefs can operate indefinitely, until, as Thoreau said, "We can lead a life of quiet desperation." He also said, "I didn't want to get to the end of my life and find I had not lived."

Life is not a dress rehearsal, folks; this is it. Right now is our chance to be happy and fulfilled.

The Book

I decided to write this book as a guide to help people recover from their unconsciously held unhelpful beliefs. I wanted others to have the experience that my clients were having: successful, lasting relationships. My hope is to cut through clinical terminology and tell you clearly what holds you back. I want to empower you, my reader, to create lasting change: not just adaptations, but real change whereby you will fully understand your conditioned chemistry.

My purpose, both in life and in this book, is to teach people how to create chemistry they can trust that will lead them to lasting, loving relationships. In order to do this, we must link our past to our present in a meaningful way. We need to understand our actions and ourselves. For decades, research has emphasized the critical impact that our early learning has upon our relationships.

During the late 1970s, psychiatrist, Dr. Eric Berne, postulated that children are born okay and that their parents create the confusion and disarray in their lives. More recently, Harvard psychologist, Dr. Jack Shonoff, tells us that the quality of our childhood relationships literally sets up chemical wiring in our brains. Our early experiences set up beliefs that create conditioned chemistry and that chemistry is tattooed into neuron communities.

Our individual brain imprinting predisposes us to certain ways of seeing relationships, certain ways of connecting with others and certain feelings of chemical attraction for specific people. Our core beliefs remain operational in our unconscious brain as drivers using an automatic gearshift — some of them operating as unconscious troublemakers — get in the way of successful relationships.

Until we understand what has programmed us, what those potential chemical tattoos are that we operate from, we don't really have a choice about whether we net positive or negative results from our decisions. We are lost, lost to ourselves primarily because of those limiting core beliefs that were formed very early in our lives. We become distanced from the awareness necessary to make satisfying personal choices about friends, lovers, colleagues and careers.

This book is meant as a resource, something you can utilize in a practical way as you read. It is my hope that as you do the exercises in this book, you will be able to reconnect with a deeper sense of yourself. I hope you will gain an understanding of how to create the relationships you want. Through an awareness of what drives you as an individual and what generates the way you relate, a profound alternative is available. My desire is to help you clarify what beliefs are working well and change those that are not. I am confident that as you put these principles into practice, your relationships will dramatically improve.

Putting Principles into Practice

The best way I know to give you an understanding of how to accomplish your relationship goals is to teach the process I use in my practice. My own personal transformation, along with that of numerous clients, will serve as exemplars.

MAE

In my case, I was 33, single and lonely. My first relationship — with my father — was unpredictable and unreliable. He appeared to favor me over my other siblings, often buying me clothing or food that he didn't get for them and taking me with him when he would go to town. But when I didn't give him what he wanted or I disagreed with him, his verbal abuse was brutal. Eventually, his abuse became physical. He was also grossly negligent towards his family. There were times when he would disappear for days or weeks, leaving us without food. In winter, we were also without heating supplies; our only source of heat was a fireplace.

My mother was terrified of being alone, was always pregnant and not able to stand up to him. She wanted me to deal with him, and when I did he turned his anger on me. So, as a little girl, I decided that he was hurtful and unpredictable, and that I couldn't depend on his love and support. My mother was also negligent. She whipped me sometimes to make me stay home from school to help her with the house and the younger children. I didn't realize then that she was terrified of being alone. I just decided that it was all up to me to get my little brothers and sisters to school, to get them something to eat or find them clothes. So I formed an initial core belief, based on what I was experiencing with both my parents, of, "I'm hurt and all alone and it's all up to me."

That belief became a limiting influence, which had a huge impact upon my adult relationships. I had men who were interested in partnering with me, but had I married any of them it would have disproved my belief that I was all alone. Then, when I found the man I couldn't live without, he was not available. In all of those relationships, I worked hard to please the man in my life, anticipating his needs, taking charge of getting what he wanted and managing our social life (operating out of the belief that it's all up to me). In both situations, I had successfully proven to myself that, "I was all alone and it was all up to me."

ALAN

Alan, a 50-year-old middle-aged man, was a respected, successful professional known for his work ethic, his tenacity, and also his temper, particularly with women. He came to see me because he was facing disciplinary actions from the state licensing agency, which could impact his ability to continue working.

Alan had just been through a nasty divorce in which his ex-wife had sued him, alleging physical abuse. He had been raised by a negligent and mostly absent addict mother and a passive, hardworking father who rarely showed any negative feelings and seemed to have unending capacity to tolerate his wife's errant behavior. Alan's father did, however, allow his feelings to show when he was at his wits end, whereupon he would call his son into the room, physically abuse his wife in his son's presence and say, "This is what you do when a woman acts like this."

This dreadful experience with Alan's parents created conditioned chemistry in his young brain that led him to become physically aggressive with women who pushed him further than his coping skills could handle. At a young age, hurt and angry because he couldn't understand why his mother was gone so much, Alan had to care for his little brother and manage their household while his father was working. His limiting core beliefs became: *It's all up to me. I'm angry. Women can't be trusted.*

Alan married a woman who literally proved his core belief about women. She was neglectful and abusive to him and he, like his father, remained quiet and passive until he could no longer contain his anger. He would then blow up and become physically aggressive with her, which resulted in legal trouble for him.

It was clear that unless Alan stayed in therapy long enough to change his core beliefs about women, his relationships with them would continue to fail. And not only would his original anger at his mother (still operating as conditioned chemistry in his unconscious brain) harm the women in his life, it would cause him to be hurt in the process. Sadly, Alan chose not to pursue therapy and continues to experience disastrous results in his intimate relationships with women.

ANDREA

Andrea was an attractive and stylish woman in her early 40s. She was recovering from recent breast cancer surgery and had become deeply introspective about the situations in her life. Having breast cancer will do that to you. Andrea wanted help to solve the discord between her husband and her son, who were not speaking to each other. Throughout her first few sessions she frequently repeated a phrase that revealed one of her core beliefs. She said, "Am I crazy or just stupid?"

As we began defining what she wanted her role to be regarding her son and her husband, it became clear to me that she was in a lot of pain about her relationship with her husband. She described him as cold, unemotional and said that he had no interest in socializing. She also portrayed him as unsupportive, lacking interest in anyone except himself. While he had taken her to some of her doctor's appointments after her breast cancer surgery, he showed no empathy, complained about being inconvenienced and didn't understand why she was upset with him.

Andrea had married at a young age to get away from an abusive home situation. As the years passed and her children grew up she became more and more lonely in the relationship, but continued to tolerate her husband's verbal abuse and controlling behavior. She was from a German Catholic community that had strong sanctions against divorce and perpetuated the idea that one should just ignore their personal problems, work hard and everything would be okay.

Andrea held the core belief: "I'm stupid and I'll never get what I want." She had been married to a man for 27 years who reinforced that belief on a regular basis. He constantly questioned her thinking, literally told her she was stupid, told her that she wanted too much and that she was never satisfied. Since her father had called her stupid as a child, she had conditioned chemistry that caused her to believe her husband, or at least to be afraid that he might be right. Andrea had developed conditioned chemistry as a child that taught her not to trust her own thinking.

I asked her to bring her husband to therapy with her. He came only when she threatened to divorce him, and his behavior confirmed that her thinking was right on target. His responses to her during the sessions were dismissive and lacked any element of empathy. He admitted calling her stupid and explained that he "didn't know what else to think of her since she had everything she needed and just couldn't seem to be satisfied."

We know from neuroscience research that verbal abuse literally kills white blood cells and lowers the immune system, which causes many kinds of physical illnesses, including cancer. I developed a contract with Andrea to value herself and trust her thinking, knowing that when she completed the contract she would be empowered to make the right decision about her marriage.

As we put principles into practice in the following chapters, I will continually cite real life examples, outline my therapeutic method and offer my techniques, which you can utilize for changing your tattooed chemistry. This process can be accomplished on your own or with the support of a professional. On your own, you can utilize the procedures in this book to determine what your early decisions were — both positive and negative.

I use examples from my own life and vignettes from some of my clients' lives to help clarify how these early decisions manifest later in relationships. Then I will give you some ideas about how you can develop an action plan to create the relationship you want, and teach you how to develop a new set of core beliefs that will create your new chemistry.

In understanding how to make this transition — the transition from lonely, struggling and discontent to connected and deeply satisfied in your relationships — it is necessary to go through a number of steps. Please hear me. I cannot emphasize enough how necessary it is to follow these steps precisely as described.

The steps will be covered in the upcoming chapters and include some theoretical background for your better understanding. I will explain the way core beliefs develop the conditioned chemistry that exerts control over your life and your relationships, and give you assessment tools for changing that chemistry. Next, I will teach you a process of tattooed chemistry removal. Finally, I will take you through strategies that permanently create new chemistry that you can trust to help you have satisfying relationships.

Everyone has deficits in their lives that handicap their ability to connect and communicate in ways that create successful relationships. This process got me to where I am today: free of fear about relationships, free of worry about whether I'll have the love and connection I desire, wholly comfortable with myself and others, and happy and deeply satisfied with my relationships.

Support

Before progressing further, it is worth considering whether you will engage in this process alone or with support. If you decide to do this process without professional help, PLEASE be careful in whom you confide. Part of the reason people seek professional help is to have the support of a neutral, un-invested party. Given that people establish relationships based on their core beliefs, the people currently in your life may not be equipped to support you changing those beliefs. Often an unbiased person can better help you establish new thought patterns and behaviors, and can better encourage your transformation without feeling threatened or envious.

If you confide the critically important information you discover through reading this book to anyone, make sure it is someone you really trust, someone who is capable of supporting you without judgment, and especially someone who will not try to rescue you or hold you back. This person must support your goals for change and desire to see you successful in your relationships. Beware of getting support from people who need you to be a certain way or need you to conform to a given set of ideals.

In Summary

What I tell my clients soon after they've walked through my door is, "You are the person with the problem and you are the person with the answer — the only person with the answer. It can't be my answer, can't be your husband's, your wife's or your friend's answer … it has to be your answer because you are the only one who truly knows you." I next ask them what they think is in the way of them having successful relationships, and I teach them how their beliefs participate in sabotaging their connection. I work to help them develop a new perspective, one in line with who they really are and what they really want, minus their conditioned beliefs. We then determine what they will need to obtain and what they will need to relinquish in order to support healthy and lasting connections with others.

The last way I support my clients is with an assessment of what evidence they will need to call this process successful. How will you know that you have achieved what you want? Sometimes we have difficulty getting to where we want to go because we don't have a picture of it.

It is human nature to gravitate towards the familiar, even when it isn't positive. My experience has taught me a couple of things that I believe to be universally true: 1) The vast majority of humans will not go towards something they cannot see; and 2) We get what we expect. So I want to help my clients, and you, my readers, create a crystal clear vision in full-color detailing what you want and expect your relationships to be. I teach you how to become intimately familiar with that picture with exercises using visual imagery.

What will your relationships look like? What will have changed in your relationships? Do you no longer sabotage yourself? One of the exercises I use is to ask my clients to visualize themselves sitting in the middle of a magic carpet surrounded by all the important people in their lives. The carpet is going to transform itself into a beautiful tapestry, flying through the air with no restraints, no limits. I tell them to assume they have complete power to obtain any new relationships they would like to add to their magic carpet, to change the ones that need change, and to give the ones they no longer want, a hot air balloon that will deliver them safely to the ground. I have them go through magazines, brochures, photographs, movies, family albums and cut out pictures, pasting them on a poster board that eventually becomes a collage of their magic carpet. Some people complete this exercise quickly and others take more time, but the magic is that they become clear about their relationships.

The insights, awareness, methods and support I offer throughout this book will help you, whether you are looking for small changes or sweeping changes. They have helped me, and I have seen them help thousands of others.

Chapter Two

The Chemistry of Relationships

*"There is no feeling more comforting and consoling
than knowing you are right next to the one you love."*
— Kay Knudsen

My guess is that you are reading this book for the same reason that many of my clients come to see me. Some aspect of your relationships — primary, social or work-related — isn't working. So I'm glad you picked up this book because the concepts and methods I teach here can have a profound effect on virtually all of your relationships.

Although all relationships are improved by the forthcoming information, my primary focus is on intimate personal relationships or primary partnerships. At the end of the day, what people want most is that one special person — the tried and true partner and friend who they can come home to. I will address how to make the right decision in choosing a life partner and how to build a satisfying, long-lasting relationship. No other decision we make in life has so much at stake.

The poet, Madeleine L'Engle says, "To marry is the biggest risk in human relations that a person can take." Our primary relationships are a big risk, and because of that we need to choose wisely. Once chosen, we need the skills to keep the relationship thriving long-term. The person you choose to partner with must be someone you can trust, someone who has your best interests at heart, someone you are safe with at your most vulnerable and someone with whom you are an equal. It is imperative that you can truly be yourself with this other person without fear of judgment or reprisal.

In my clinical practice, I have successfully guided thousands of couples through the challenges of their relationships. I feel I can speak with some authority about what I see as the primary types of relationship problems, and I can teach you what I do in my practice to help individuals find and keep appropriate partnerships.

In this chapter, I will discuss the importance of relationships — not only their importance to our emotional wellbeing, but their importance to our physical wellbeing. Then I will cover a little about the cultural factors that currently affect us, and the treadmill that most of us live on that interferes with successful connecting.

I also want to give you a better understanding of core beliefs, those early repetitive thought patterns that get unconsciously imprinted or tattooed in our brains, those early beliefs that all people form based on what they experienced in their childhood environment. These beliefs, which literally become our brain chemistry, play the leading role in determining our relationship patterns. They are the controlling force, the tattoo in our choices about partners, and they ubiquitously dictate where and when we feel the chemistry.

Lastly, I will outline the four major categories of relationship issues I see in my practice. These categories are where most people find themselves struggling, and it bears looking at what they are and how people create these patterns. If asked, most people can say what isn't working in their relationships, at least in a general sense. With more detailed information about different types of relationship patterns, you will be able to identify your problems more specifically. This is a wonderful starting point for unraveling and reconstructing what isn't working.

The Importance of Relationships

When all is said and done, and you look back on your life, what you will find is that satisfying relationships will have been the best indicator of happiness. The quality of your relationships and the quality of the connections you had with other people will be what really mattered. And the most important of these connections will have been with a primary partner.

Research tells us that our brain has a stronger chemical reaction, even if we are unconscious, to the touch of a partner than to anyone else. Our partner is that one critically important person who, to a large extent, determines our wellbeing. Knowing how to understand the chemistry we feel for others can translate into having and maintaining a satisfying long-term partnership. Understanding chemistry is crucial for happiness.

Given the importance of primary relationships, it is no surprise that challenges with a relationship is the number one issue people bring to therapy. Having a stable, fulfilling, intimate relationship is pervasively people's top priority. It is the area where most people want, and most need, change, as it is the area that can cause them the most heartache or give them the most joy.

When people feel close to others, they are happier and healthier. John Cacioppo, a neuroscientist at the University of Chicago and co-author of a book, *Loneliness: Human Nature and the Need for Social Connection,* writes about the impact of human connection on health and wellbeing. His research indicates that, from the beginning of history, we humans have learned to depend on our families and our tribes for protection. We feel safer when we are closely connected to other people because being isolated or alone equates to death in our genetic memory.

Historically, shunning was considered a severe form of punishment, as individuals could rarely survive without the interdependence of their group. We know that children need a lot of attention and will actually create negative attention rather than endure a lack of attention. The need for others is literally wired into our brains; it is part of our chemistry.

Consequently, that painful feeling known as loneliness is actually a chemically imprinted prompt to reconnect with others, and it is just as powerful as hunger, thirst or pain. It is literally part of our genetic lineage, a hereditary survival mechanism. Throughout millennia we have been programmed chemically to believe that loneliness signals something important for the survival of our genes — we need to connect with others to survive and to feel okay.

Cacioppo elaborates further on how relationships affect our health. He says, "Social isolation has an impact on health comparable to high blood pressure, obesity, lack of exercise or smoking," clearly telling us that a lack of connected relationships is detrimental to our wellbeing. He goes on to say that, "Loneliness shows up in measurements of stress hormones, immune function and cardiovascular function. Lonely adults consume more alcohol and get less exercise than those who are not lonely. Their diet is higher in fat, their sleep is less efficient and they report more daytime fatigue."

Intuitively, we can feel how our life force is compromised when our relationships are lacking or unsatisfying. Further, in the academic literature there are ample studies that correlate quality and low quantity of relationships to increased risk of death. Social isolation, literally, is a risk factor for early mortality.

All in all, the importance of relationships should not be underestimated. When you think about improving your health by losing weight, quitting smoking, working out more, eating healthier or getting more sleep, how many of us have "find or improve relationships" on the list?

Society and the Treadmill

Relationships are always predicated on what's happening in society. Our culture dictates the rules we follow and the roles we play: the dos and don'ts when it comes to relationships. What is acceptable at one point in time, or within a given society, may not be acceptable at a different point in time or within a different culture. To look effectively at relationships, we have to contextualize them against what is happening in the society around us. This applies not only to cultural norms about relationships, but to society at large and how it supports, or not, connections with other people.

Historically, groups of people lived separated from each other, and individuals within a group were dependent on that family or tribe for most everything. Partnerships developed through arranged marriages as part of necessity and survival. The termination of a marriage was rare because society didn't allow for it. Lifespans were short and marriages maintained due to economic need. Success in relationships was dependent on fate or a strong ability to work with what you were given, but choice, and certainly chemistry, rarely played a part.

Our current culture offers a myriad of modern choices. We can choose our own partners based on attraction, we can marry young or old, we can partner with the same sex or the opposite sex. Women are able to support themselves independent from men, couples can choose to live together unmarried, and there is far less economic pressure to be partnered. We can surf online and choose from hundreds of possible partners. If the relationship we currently have isn't working, we can trade it in for a new and better model.

These kinds of options did not exist even 50 years ago. The revolution in our social norms around relationships is staggering and a direct reflection of the change in our overall culture. Things in our society (including relationships) have become disposable, the pace of life frenetic, the value of connection diminished and the emphasis on materialism paramount.

I once heard an author talking on a morning radio show about understanding society through listening to people's cocktail conversations. Essentially, what people talk about when newly introduced says volumes about the culture's values. It used to be that at a social gathering, when people were introduced, they would politely ask, "Whose son are you?" meaning who are you related to and who are your connections? At that point in time, relationships and families were more prized culturally.

Now at a cocktail party, the standard query would be, "What do you do?" meaning what to you do for work or money? From this information, a general sense of economic status is derived and individuals judged based on material worth. This paradigm is wholly representative of a change in cultural norms — from people being of highest value, to money and material things being of highest value.

This current emphasis on money and materialism has most of us living life on a treadmill, endlessly running to create the income and lifestyle we are culturally conditioned to want. We place value on getting, spending, convenience and immediate gratification. While I'm not writing a sociological book here, there is no question in my mind that many of my clients are just too tired and too stressed from the schedules they keep to summon the amount of reflective energy they need to problem solve in their relationships.

Americans work more hours and vacation less than any other country on Earth. We have been programmed to believe that having bigger and better material things is more important than being and becoming our authentic satisfied self. It's a huge lie. These habitual work ethics, and the striving for material goods that dominate our current culture, undermine the time and energy needed to have and sustain successful relationships.

Catherine, one of my clients, said it very succinctly: "Time for relationships? You've got to be kidding. Between work and the kids, all their activities, the bills and the house, there is barely time left over to think, let alone pay attention to my husband." This is an essential part of the problem. Without time to think and reflect, we are running on autopilot. That gives our unconscious beliefs the power to run our lives, it gives our conditioned chemistry control and our results are not consciously chosen.

What Underlies Chemistry? Core Beliefs.

How do you choose a partner? What makes one person more attractive than another? What is compatibility based on, and what kinds of similarities bode well for long-term relationships? Is it looks? Common interests? What about lifestyle and religion? Dating services have lengthy questionnaires that match their clients with that perfect someone. However, the truth of whom we choose, are attracted to or have chemistry with is actually based on something outside of our awareness. You might think you want a tall, athletic, reliable partner who is accomplished and loves to travel, but the partner you are attracted to is not based on what you consciously think or what you consciously want.

Whom you are attracted to is based on the conditioned chemistry of your unconscious belief system and specifically on your core beliefs. These core beliefs are a series of decisions you made as a very young child based on your environment and the people in it. How people treated you, how they talked to you and the behavioral examples of those around you produced your understandings about relationships. These understandings created beliefs that became a part of your unconscious, literally a part of your brain chemistry. Then, as you matured, you made decisions and felt attraction based on the unconscious beliefs, the conditioned chemistry generated by your unconscious.

For example, let's consider Laura.

LAURA

She is a beautiful and intelligent young woman with a history of failed relationships. Laura was partnered with several young men during her 20s, but they all remained aloof and uncommitted until she finally ended the relationships and went looking for someone else.

Recently, Laura attended a social reception. There were numerous attractive, available young men in attendance, successful professionals that she might connect with. But as she surveyed the room, she kept coming back to a ruggedly handsome young man leaning up against the wall by the bar. He was alone, drinking a beer and checking out the girls with a crooked smile. Although he ignored Laura, she was inexplicably attracted to this "bad boy," the one outside the group. He was reminiscent of her last boyfriend and something told her she should ignore him, but she felt a strong attraction and thought he could be different. She was so strongly attracted to him that she couldn't focus on anyone else. Laura felt so much chemistry for this bad boy that she didn't give the others much thought.

Looking at the situation from a distance, we can see Laura being attracted to the same type of guy she has failed with before, and the question is why? Why does she find herself drawn to the same type of man over and over, even though she keeps experiencing failure? Human beings are drawn towards what is familiar, whether it is good for us or not. What has been tattooed into Laura's unconscious? What kind of conditioned chemistry is driving her attraction?

Laura grew up with a father who was an alcoholic and a loner. She loved him very much, and he was her first powerful connection with a man. Laura's father often ignored her as a child and was too drunk to be present or connect. Nevertheless, Laura loved her father deeply. Her father's behavior created beliefs in Laura's unconscious that she didn't deserve to be loved or attended to. The unconscious beliefs she formed about that relationship are now underneath her feelings of chemical attraction.

As an adult, she is unconsciously attracted to men who will behave in ways that recreate the same feelings she felt with her father. Out of her awareness, and to her detriment, she is looking for a man she can love intensely, but expect nothing from in return.

Like Laura, most of us don't realize that our unconscious

patterns — our conditioned brain chemistry — underlie our attraction to others. The beliefs and early decisions stored in our brain play the single most important role in who we choose as friends and partners. And, to a large extent, this brain chemistry dictates whether our relationships will be successful.

ELIZABETH AND TODD

Elizabeth is a perfect example of how core beliefs work. At her core she believed, "I'm not good enough." She came to my office reporting fatigue, anxiety and feeling disconnected in her relationships. At 36, she had been married for 14 years and had three children: two girls and a boy. Her life was maxed out with a full-time job as an art teacher, a part-time job coaching soccer, an art studio, a sizeable home and yard, and a family dog all under her purview. Her anxiety centered around not having enough time to get things done, and not doing a good enough job at any of them.

Just listening to Elizabeth, I felt tired. She was up by 6:00 in the morning, caring for children, then driving carpool and getting to her job. After work there were dinner and kids' activities, the cleaning, the bills and the housework. Her day whirled by without stopping until she fell into bed around midnight.

Her husband, Todd, who was also employed full-time and coached as well, helped with their children and their home, but they often argued about household chores and parenting responsibilities. After some years, these arguments began to chip away at their relationship and they began distancing themselves from each other.

Elizabeth's life wasn't working. She couldn't find time to do her own personal artwork and felt she was not doing a good job anywhere, either at home or at work. Feeling distant from her husband, she believed she just wasn't a good enough wife, that somehow she just couldn't do what was needed and even if she did, it wouldn't be good enough.

Elizabeth's husband loved her dearly, but he teased her about not getting things done. Occasionally, she saw through his teasing. Todd's comments sometimes hurt her deeply and reminded her of messages she had received from her parents. Elizabeth had married and set up a lifestyle with a man who reinforced her core belief, "I'm not good enough." No matter how hard she worked, it just wasn't enough. Anxious to perform and to please, angry and exhausted from trying, she finally sought help.

The Different Relationship Types

People have a variety of different core beliefs that create their individual experiences of chemistry and result in particular relationship patterns. In my practice, I see the same basic relationship patterns over and over again. These relationship patterns, or types, are the result of a given set of core beliefs working together to form a pattern of who you are attracted to and how the relationship dynamics play out. You may identify with one particular type and find it useful to understand how you, like many others, have developed this relationship pattern. The beliefs that underlie these patterns, left untreated, can cause the failure of a relationship, something this book is aimed at helping you avoid.

1. Perpetually Un-partnered

This person wants a relationship, but they can't seem to stay connected to anybody. They experience a significant deficit in the neurochemistry that seeks connection; they just aren't attracted to anyone and no one is attracted to them. They can appear to be asexual and are sometimes thought to be gay or bisexual, but that is not the case. They might enjoy sex with someone, but there is nothing that really sparks their interest in connecting. Additionally, they can lack the capacity for emotional bonding and have no conditioned chemistry (core beliefs) to cause them to actually attach to another person.

This person will often say things like "I really need to find someone" or "I guess I'm not likeable or something. " As a child, they did not receive the emotional connection they needed from either parent and over a period of time they decided they were not loveable. What else could a child decide? Then, in order to deal with the loneliness and pain, they went on to decide, "I'm all alone. I don't need anyone." An example would be someone like my client Keith.

KEITH

Keith, 45, came to see me saying, "I'm not sure what's wrong, but I'm just not happy." Raised by parents who never played with him or showed him any affection, Keith reported that he had no memory of them holding him, reading to him or hugging him. He was an only child and remembers spending a lot of time in his room alone, playing with toys, and as he got older, reading. His parents took good care of his physical needs, but were unavailable emotionally.

Additionally, Keith was sensitive and creative. He was not popular in school, not very good at sports and was always the last one chosen in any competitive event. People encountering this kind of experience often decide "There's something wrong with me, no matter how hard I try, I can't win. I'm not liked." What they experience in school is similar to what they experienced as a child - rejection, isolation. They move through their life with low energy, cynicism, and a chronic feeling of unhappiness or even hopelessness that can turn into full-blown clinical depression.

2. Replicating the Tattoo

Like the woman who marries for the second time and once again chooses an alcoholic, this individual is continuously attracted to, and engages with, the same kind of partner who didn't work out for them before. Comparable to Laura in my previous example (who had been raised by an alcoholic father), their conditioned chemistry — what has been tattooed into their unconscious — keeps them attracted to the same type of person, who is not viable for a meaningful relationship. This pattern can develop with individuals who grew up watching their parents engage in a highly dysfunctional relationship. It can also happen when the parents, for whatever reason, are not emotionally available to the child.

Our instinct is to gravitate towards what is familiar. If dysfunction has been modeled and tattooed into our unconscious, without making change to our beliefs we will be continually stuck on our default programming, replicating the tattoo.

The core beliefs that support this kind of relationship pattern are: "I'm hurt and all alone." Like Laura, whose father was emotionally unavailable because of his alcoholism, people with this core belief were hurt or neglected emotionally by the first man or woman in their life, and they became accustomed to living in a primary relationship where their emotional needs were unmet. Since our brain chemistry adapts to the environment in which we are living, they did not develop the ability (the conditioned chemistry) to connect emotionally with others. So they are accustomed to tolerating dysfunction at a high level. They literally don't have any expectations for happiness in relationships and keep choosing partners who are not emotionally available to them.

3. The Closed Heart

The individual with the closed heart may feel attraction for others, get involved, even get married, but the relationships lack connection. Whatever happened in their early environment, this person never developed the ability to make an intimate connection. Rather, they actually developed conditioned chemistry, which prevents them from connecting. They can attract partners — sometimes appropriate partners — but the relationships lack emotional content and their partners are often unsatisfied, lonely and eventually find themselves wanting out of the relationship.

People with this kind of relationship pattern have core beliefs such as, "I can't be me" or "My needs don't matter." This person would have been ignored or punished as a child when they expressed their feelings and would have decided that feelings are irrelevant, they don't matter, or possibly, feelings are bad, they cause trouble. These individuals see showing emotion as a sign of weakness or as a waste of time or as a troublemaker.

I'm reminded of the father whose wife and children were hurt, sad and angry at his coldness, saying to him, "We know that you love us, but we can't feel it." And his response was to say, "I'm sorry, I wish I could feel the way you need me to, but I just can't." Some people with this kind of condition were either abused or ignored as a child when they displayed their feelings, so they literally learned (their brain set up conditioned chemistry) not to feel. The neural pathways that provide the ability to emotionally connect simply are not there.

4. Unglued

This category involves the couple that has been married for many years, but their chemistry ceases to motivate them to stay together. Perhaps they had children who are now grown and living on their own. Now it's just the two of them again. One or both of them has changed, perhaps dealt with their limiting core beliefs, and is no longer drawn to the other by that early conditioned chemistry. So unless they have developed a strong friendship in which there is admiration, respect and common interests, their relationship is in peril.

The unglued couple has core beliefs that might look like my clients, Jack and Sarah.

JACK AND SARAH

Jack held the core belief: "I'm weak and not very capable." Sarah's core belief was: "It's all up to me and I won't get what I want until …" During the early years in their marriage, Sarah was the dominant partner in the relationship and took charge of everything: the house, the finances, the parenting, the social calendar, everything. Then as she approached mid-life, she began to feel tired, really tired. She began telling Jack that she needed him to step up and take more responsibility, to take some of the load off her. He didn't. She asked him to change for several years, with no success.

When Sarah first came to see me, she had already been to see an attorney. She said, "I'm exhausted. I'm tired of being responsible for absolutely everything and I feel like my husband is just another one of the kids. I feel like I'm done, but I hate the thought of divorce." Sarah was changing her core belief. She had come to the realization that it wasn't right for her to do it all. In the beginning, she had married a man who would give her the control she wanted, but when she finally wore herself out, she wanted him to change and if Jack couldn't change, the chances for this marriage to continue were questionable.

Jack wasn't happy with her either. In one of our sessions, he looked at her indignantly and said, "You've changed, I haven't. It's not my fault!" Jack needed someone to lean on, someone who would provide the strength and decision-making process he felt inadequate to provide. So he wasn't getting what he wanted from her either. The glue — the conditioned chemistry that had brought Jack and Sarah together — had lost its holding power.

These categories can overlap, but they are the predominant ones that I see repeatedly in my practice. Successful partnering is all about emotional connection and core beliefs that expect happy, healthy relationships. There is however, one exception to this and that would involve the people in categories 1 and 3: those lonely unfortunates who don't have the conditioned chemistry to connect or have it so buried that even dynamite cannot break down their wall.

A person who is unable to make an emotionally intimate attachment is much better off in a relationship with a partner who has the same "condition." I say condition because it is generally unnatural to the human condition to be emotionally unconnected. The unfortunate result of this kind of union, though, is that if they have children they may perpetuate the condition, the inability to emotionally, intimately connect.

I have found over the years in my practice that it is nearly impossible for someone to give emotional connection if they didn't receive it from a significant caregiver during the early years of their life.

In Summary

This chapter was aimed at giving you a foundation for concepts that will be discussed throughout this book. A great starting point, when looking to change what isn't working in your relationships, is to think about them in terms of the four components I have just outlined. First, how important are your relationships? Are they affecting your overall health and wellbeing? Are they a priority? Second, what is happening in your life that interferes with putting time and attention into your relationships? Are you too busy, too tired to put energy where it is needed? What aspects of your life — from your values to your routines — impede having the rich, nurturing relationships you want? Third, you must begin to think about what is operating unconsciously in your brain that drives your conditioned chemistry, your attraction to certain people. And lastly, how does that conditioned chemistry result in a relationship pattern that either is, or isn't, working to your satisfaction?

In the following chapters I will take you through a process of more deeply understanding the conditioned chemistry of your core beliefs, understanding how to change that conditioned chemistry, and understanding how to create and reinforce healthier belief systems. These steps are all aimed at allowing you to experience deeply satisfying and fulfilling relationships. Both nature: your genetic background, and nurture: your early environment, are intricately linked and play an important role in the development of your conditioned chemistry, and thus your relationships. The next chapter will explore those roles.

Chapter Three

The Nature and Nurture of Tattooed Chemistry

"You have to do your own growing
no matter how tall your grandfather was."
— Abraham Lincoln

As young girl growing up in poverty, neglect and abuse, I learned to see the world in a certain way. In the midst of my extremely compromised circumstances, my father, paternal grandmother, teachers and church leaders singled me out for my intelligence and creative talent. Important people in my life had high expectations of me and I was given a lot of positive attention, which obscured some of the limiting beliefs I was forming about my relationships and my life. Consequently, when I left home I took with me a mixture of ideas, and as my life unfolded and circumstances changed, I unconsciously recreated that mixture. I had some very strong chemical tattoos about relationships and about the world. I knew one way of living in a family — a very harsh and dysfunctional one — but I had also seen thought-provoking glimpses of a different, better way.

How then did I — a young girl from devastating circumstances — overcome my early conditioning and prosper as a healthy, functioning adult? And, how did I attain a successful, long-term marriage enduring, now, for more than 30 years?

I reached a place where I realized that I didn't have the answers I needed and I sought help. I feel lucky that my life experiences and my personal perseverance landed me in therapy and helped me work to change my limited and destructive early conditioning, resulting in the wonderful life I now have.

I cannot say that out of my numerous siblings (18 of us in total from my father's two marriages) very many were able to flourish, but a few did. As I looked at my siblings, whom I love very much, I wanted to understand why some overcame our circumstances and others didn't. I wanted to understand what drives us and what determines our level of happiness and our ability to create successful relationships.

In the first few years after I had left home, I periodically returned and convinced various younger siblings to leave and live with other families. Much to my dismay, they only lasted a short time before they went back. I couldn't understand why they didn't want something better. I finally realized that I had different expectations based on my core beliefs.

In the process of working to understand human nature, I studied a number of different theories about personality development. John Doyle and Dr. Valerie Chang — my own therapists — influenced my thinking with their emphasis on transactional analysis (TA). The foundation for my professional orientation is based on transactional analysis and working with core beliefs, but my therapeutic approach is a combination of TA, psychodynamic and cognitive-behavioral techniques. Along with the focus on TA and core beliefs, I did my graduate work in clinical psychology, where I incorporated an understanding of genetic/neurological components that form our personality and affect our behavior. These two concepts — inherited genetic traits and environmentally conditioned chemistry — are the focus of this chapter.

My goal here is not to tire you, the reader, with too much theoretical detail, but I do feel it is important to give you enough background that you can understand my therapeutic process as it is detailed throughout the remainder of the book.

Nature Versus Nurture

In the social sciences and medicine, there was a great psychological debate that raged over the last half of the 20th century. This debate focused on trying to understand what factors determine a person's personality and behavior. Movies like *Trading Places* (1983), with Dan Akroyd and Eddie Murphy, and books like *The Third Twin* (1996), by Ken Follett, profiled the dilemma regarding what determines a human's behavior, his/her genetics or his/her environment.

Extensive twin studies at academic institutions such as the University of Minnesota have provided supporting evidence for the genetic component, while extensive social science research has established support for the effects of environment. This debate has leveled off in recent years with most doctors and psychologists conceding that personality and behavior are a combination of both genetics and environment. First it's nature, then nurture, and the two become inextricably entwined.

Nature or Genetic Lineage

Just as we inherit physical characteristics such as height, weight, eye color, dimples, freckles, a straight hairline or a widow's peak, we also inherit aspects of our temperaments, our personalities. As a child, we come into this world with a predetermined set of genetic tendencies inherited from our biological parents that make some of us outgoing and others shy, some of us easy to anger while others remain mellow. Some of us are more aggressive and dominant, while others are more cautious and passive.

Certain personalities need lots of stimulation and change, while others want things to remain the same. We can observe babies and see that some are adventurous and inquiring, while others are cautious and hesitant. Some children are basically content while others are easily agitated and irritable. Personality can be assessed in many ways, from social behaviors to emotional expression, but everyone is born with the basics of their temperament.

Research on inherited personality traits comes largely out of identical twin studies. When twins are raised in different families, with different socioeconomic levels and in different cultural milieus, they still have strikingly similar preferences and traits. This means that the genetic components of their make-up can be empirically examined because the similarities in their characters cannot be attributed to similarities in upbringing or environment.

Not only are standard personality traits inherited, but distortions, dysfunctions and abnormalities as well. There are genetic studies that have identified specific genes related to specific disorders. Attention deficit disorder, for example, seems to be genetically related, as well as panic disorders and schizophrenia. Bi-polar disorder has a strong genetic correlate. These inherited genetic traits help form a foundation that significantly contributes to the development of our personalities and who we choose as partners.

Nurture and Beliefs Systems

Research further shows us that what happens to us as children — especially in our formative years — lays an additional foundation for long-term intellectual, physical and emotional development. What happens to a child in the first three or four years of life builds on their genetic predispositions and determines, to a considerable extent, how intelligent they will become and whether or not they will develop learning problems and mood disorders. At the risk of having the text become too clinical, I want to give you some specific information about what scientists have learned from their studies because this will provide you a better understanding of how beliefs are formed and maintained. This will include some basic information on the impact of environment, core beliefs and brain imprinting, as well as the impact of neglect and abuse, including domestic violence and substance abuse.

Environment

A child begins trying to make sense of his or her world soon after birth. Initially, the child is totally engaged in a symbiotic relationship with the mother and does not recognize himself/herself as a separate entity. Between the ages of one and three, this intensely symbiotic state begins to diminish, but the awareness that the people caring for them (mother, father, other) have total power over their lives is well established.

Shakespeare said, "Children see their parents as God's generals." At some point very early in a child's life it understands … "If they don't feed and protect me, I will die. Therefore, these people are all-powerful, all-knowing. So how they treat me, how they feel about me and what they say about me must be true."

It is clear that we decide how best to survive based on how we are treated and what is going on in our environment. And based on what we decide, we develop patterns of behavior and choose relationships to support our decisions. We can begin to observe these behaviors as early as age three. These survival behavior patterns translate into beliefs that we use to relate to the larger world and were developed based on the experiences we had primarily with the powerful people in our lives — usually our parents.

From the way we learn to survive, we develop powerful driving beliefs about the way life is going to be, about others and about ourselves. These are intense, passionate beliefs that can cause us to make absolute decisions, which we then begin to unconsciously live out in our everyday lives.

We have all heard stories about children who made decisions such as "I'm smart" or "I can be anything I want," and go on to become successful professionals. It is also true that children make decisions like "I'm not lovable," "No matter what I do, I can't win" or "I'm a burden," that then choose partners who, in some powerful way, confirm those beliefs. Negative core beliefs can lead them to unfulfilled, sometimes even failed or self-destructive, lives.

From the experiences we have in our early environments, we all make the absolute best choices possible. With limited understanding and no control over our surroundings, we make the best decisions we were capable of making about our worlds, our connection with others and ourselves. These decisions, which become etched into our brain chemistry, can, when we reach adulthood, really cause us difficulty. Just as the toys we played with as children don't suit us as grownups, some of the understandings we formed as children don't serve us as adults, and in fact, can prevent us from choosing healthy relationships.

Core Beliefs

In childhood we have many experiences and form many beliefs, but every individual has a set of predominate beliefs that we call core beliefs. These are the beliefs that have been reinforced more consistently or have been formed in relation to a high degree of emotion. These are our most dominant beliefs and the ones that direct our behaviors and relationships.

These beliefs vary from individual to individual, but in general, are a composite of ideas we have formed in relation to what we were told as children. This might look like a child being told over and over that what they do "isn't good enough." This could be said directly, or reinforced indirectly, but either way can result in a core belief like, "I'm not good enough; no matter how much I do or how much I achieve, it'll never be enough."

This core belief would likely be coupled with other core beliefs, depending on the individual's experience. If the parents and caregivers criticized the child and reinforced a need to be perfect, the child may develop an additional belief around, "I need to be perfect and please others." These beliefs are formed in relation to our experiences and are a way to survive and respond to our environments in order to receive love and approval. If love and approval are contingent on being perfect, then we begin to believe this is the truth of how we have to be. These beliefs dictate our behaviors and control the outcomes of virtually every aspect of our lives — from how we manage our money to the partners we choose.

From our early experiences we begin to get an idea of who we are in the world. If, for example, our primary caretakers are always upset with us and push us away, we might determine that there is something wrong with us and we are unlovable. If someone develops a core belief from childhood that says, "I am unlovable," this core belief can play out in adulthood and interfere with successful relationships. An individual might try to find a partner, he/she might date and date and wonder why it never works out, unaware that some core belief is potentially working in opposition to their goal. One who believes, "I am unlovable," might unconsciously choose a partner who is incapable of loving, thereby supporting their internal belief.

We all have experiences in our lives where we desire something and work hard to achieve it without success. We can't consciously understand why it is that way. Our core beliefs are operating without our awareness, and are at the root of the results we see.

Brain Imprinting

We can all understand that experiences in childhood likely translate to beliefs about the world. My childhood experiences taught me to believe that life is hard, that I couldn't trust anyone and that I was all alone. I had positive beliefs as well, but they were not the ones I needed to change in adulthood. They were not blocking my happiness.

So, how do these core beliefs establish themselves in our minds during our development process? As children, when we interact, we respond to given circumstances with a thought process in our brain, a literal firing of neurons between different points. This firing of neurons from the limbic (feeling) brain and the neo-cortex (the thinking brain) structures the neurons into a community. And what is a neuron community? It's a group of thought formations that becomes imprinted and develops a neural pathway. How do they impede us later in life? How does appropriate responding as a child become conditioned chemistry that gets in the way of our adult functioning? What really are these chemistry tattoos, as I have euphemistically termed them?

Technology doesn't yet allow us to measure intellectual capacity in babies, but current research indicates that everything we experience creates neurochemical reactions in the brain. What we repeatedly experience creates neural pathways and neuron communities in our brains, which then generate beliefs and behaviors that operate throughout our lives. What we see in the relationship between our caregivers is the relationship we learn as we grow up and then re-create as adults.

I realize that a discussion about brain chemistry may sound rather cold and uninviting, but it is a key part of our reality and to leave it unaccounted for would be a true disservice to you, my reader. So hang in there with me, it will start to make sense in ensuing chapters.

The physical, emotional and intellectual experiences that children have during their early years are imprinted within the structure of the brain. The brain seems to assume that if the child keeps repeating a response in relation to its environment, that response promotes survival and should be imprinted in the brain for safekeeping. The brain then begins to help the child adapt to its environment by strengthening the neural connections that are used repeatedly and by eliminating those that are infrequently used.

The brain literally tattoos these frequently-experienced responses into permanent core beliefs that will operate indefinitely without intervention and generate specific outcomes. This, of course, impacts us for the rest of our life. These core beliefs support, even generate, behaviors that helped us survive in childhood, but have the potential to sabotage our success in adulthood.

We can all resonate with the plethora of motivational speakers and self-help books that abound with talk about beliefs equating to outcomes. Concepts like, "What the mind of man can conceive and believe, it can achieve," or "You must *believe* in yourself in order to achieve anything" are common colloquialisms. But what we believe about relationships is what we create, because it is what we have imprinted in our brains.

The Impact of Neglect and Abuse

Early abuse and neglect are extremely damaging to a child's way of understanding the world. What they witness and experience create specific thoughts and feelings that form core beliefs and leave an imprint on the neural pathways of that child's brain. Once formed, these brain cognitions can predispose them to depression, anxiety or thought disorders. And it can predispose them to choose abusive or neglectful relationships.

Traumatized children experience developmental delays, including cognitive, emotional, language, motor and socialization. They develop physical and psychological problems that manifest themselves throughout their lives. Many of them, as they grow into adulthood, have poor academic performance, delinquent or criminal behaviors, increased prevalence of alcohol or drug dependence, significant difficulties in personal and professional relationships, and worst of all, they grow up to repeat abusive and neglectful parenting behaviors, tragically transferring the cycle of violence onto future generations.

Brain development proceeds amazingly fast in the first three years of life and children need to have lots of positive stimulation and be protected from abuse and neglect. By age three, the child's brain has twice as many neural connections as an adult's and the first 12 years of life are the prime time for the development of conditioned chemistry.

Cognition — our ability to correctly perceive, process and act upon what we experience in our world — is critical to our survival, but emotion is the looking glass, the filter, through which we view our world. Emotion colors every thought, every activity, every relationship and every response. The emotional centers in the brain are so powerful that they can take charge of other brain activities, like learning.

When we are afraid, angry, sad or hurt, the brain's chemical processes prevent us from concentrating. When emotions are running high, our heart rate increases, blood pressure increases, our blood leaves the brain and flows to our appendages so that we can respond to the threat with a fight or flight response and we literally are unable to think effectively. How many times have you said, "I wish I had thought to say that, or not to say that?"

In order to learn, a child must feel secure. A child's sense of security depends on trust — trust in the parents, the all-powerful caregivers. Without that trust, the learning process becomes a prisoner of the child's emotions; learning and memory become diminished by the chronic state of anxiety in which the child lives.

If children can trust, they develop beliefs that, in turn, develop behavior patterns based on spontaneity, autonomy and intimacy. When children cannot trust, the opposite experiences of compulsive, addictive, anxiety-based ritualistic behaviors develop.

Toddlers, by age three, have reached almost 90 percent of their brain's development, and to reach each stage of development optimally, the brain requires good health, good nutrition, security, stability and a massive amount of stimulation. Children require an enormous amount of time, attention, guidance and patience. My own childhood had only one of those elements. I had lots of stimulation because there were always so many of us milling around; we also had constant stimulation as a result of the violence frequently visited upon our family by our father and the resulting fear, anger, sadness and frustration.

The children in my family could not develop emotional trust because their environment was too unpredictable, not to mention deprived in terms of the basic needs of nutrition and shelter. Interestingly, though, it appears to me that most of my siblings are sufficiently intelligent. It was our lack of emotional intelligence — the anxiety, the paranoia, the depression and defensiveness that caused many of us problems.

Research confirms that failure to properly nourish a child, inflicting physical pain and verbally abusing a child or simply ignoring the emotional needs of a small child cause trauma to the brain. Physical, emotional and sensory deprivation tends to bring about or encourage organic changes. If certain systems in the brain stem are not sufficiently stimulated, degenerative changes in the nerve cells may follow. We know, for example, that positive physical contact raises endorphin levels in our brain, which creates a number of positive chemical, physical and emotional reactions ... lowers the heart rate, lowers blood pressure, relieves tension.

Conversely, physical and emotional abuse creates negative chemicals in our brain that result in psychological problems and learning difficulties. Abuse and neglect also create low self-esteem and limit a person's ability to thrive. In other words, physical and emotional deprivation can, at its worst, have a fatal outcome. I don't know if the abuse and deprivation that I experienced in my family caused fatal outcomes, but it certainly took a heavy toll on many lives.

Domestic Violence

Domestic violence constitutes the single most significant precursor for the maltreatment of children ending in fatalities, with substance abuse and addiction being the primary causes of domestic violence. The number of adults in our society who, at some point in their lives, have been neglected and/or physically, sexually or emotionally assaulted is significant and grossly underreported.

Millions of children witness acts of domestic violence each year, and children seeing a parent or sibling being battered experience the same level of trauma as the person being abused. Lab results show that they experience the same level of stress-related brain chemicals as the person being battered. The impact upon neural pathways, which influence cognitive and emotional abilities, appears to be the same.

Substance Abuse

Substance abusing parents use their resources to pay for drugs, alcohol and partying, which often results in lack of food, clothing, shelter and adequate medical care for the children. Lack of guidance and supervision from these parents causes psychological damage and often places the children in dangerous physical jeopardy. Children trying to grow up in homes where their parents abuse drugs and alcohol are three times likelier to be abused and five times likelier to be neglected.

Sexual abuse is not uncommon among these children since they are frequently exposed to non-related addicted adults. Worse, estimates indicate that up to 45 percent of all incest reported cases involve a parent that uses drugs in some form. Most cases still go unreported because of the shame and conflicted feelings the child experiences for the abusing parent.

Children of substance abusers are at extremely high risk of developing their own substance abuse problems or choosing a partner with substance abuse problems, later in life. First, we now know that alcoholism is highly inheritable and, secondly, as these children enter adolescence they often begin using alcohol and drugs to cope with their low self-esteem, depression, anxiety and traumatic memories.

Dr. John Gottman refers to these coping mechanisms as "enduring vulnerabilities;" they are a result of the child's victimization. Chronic and constant use of substances has been role modeled for them since birth and they are desensitized to the damaging possibilities looming in their own future. Their early use of substances can lead to all sorts of maladaptive behaviors that cause them to choose abusive relationships and/ or to come in contact with the legal system for delinquent or criminal actions. Tragically, substance abuse can impact children before birth. More than half a million babies born in this country each year have been overexposed to alcohol and drugs by their mother while still in the womb.

As terrible as my own childhood circumstances were, I was fortunate in some ways; we were not sexually abused (as far as I know) and my mother didn't drink or use. Also, I lived in rural areas where the Christian teachings of local churches still exercised considerable influence on the behavior of individuals in the community. The majority of my extended family is made up of moral, responsible people committed to their families and their communities. Only one of my siblings — out of the 18 who lived — became chronically engaged in criminal behavior. Some of us are teetotalers, some drink rarely, some drink regularly, some have issues with substance abuse. Few of us are good at managing money, we tend to either hoard it or spend it all, and most of us have had significant difficulties in our relationships at some point.

The impact of abuse and neglect on children is enormous and when I look at the emotional, physical, financial and relational condition of my brothers and sisters, the picture is clearly illuminated. Our parents didn't have a strong foundation to build upon. They, too, were the product of their nature/nurture experience.

Transactional Analysis

Transactional Analysis (TA) was developed in the 1950s when Sigmund Freud's theories still dominated much of the psychological community's thinking. Replacing Freud's psycho-sexual theories of the individual as a series of internal states or drivers — namely the Id, Ego and Superego — Eric Berne proposed a focus on interactions instead of internal states with an ego composed of Child, Adult and Parent aspects. Berne looked at an individual's interactions, which he termed "transactions," analyzing them in relation to the individual's developmental history. He postulated that the individual developed a "life script" through a process of imbedded beliefs as a result of his/her various "transactions."

Eric Berne, Claude Steiner and others, in their further development of the theory of Transactional Analysis, concluded that children make compelling, existential life-shaping decisions about themselves, others and the way life is going to be, based on these transactions and the bulk of these decisions or beliefs are made by the time children are between three and five years old. They make these decisions based upon the information passed down from their parents, what is going on in their environment on a regular basis, their ability to think and what they decide to believe.

Transactional Analysis understands that this early existential decision-making is of monumental importance in all our perceptions and choices ... how we live, work and interact with others, how we choose our partners, our careers and, ultimately, how long we will live.

Transactional Analysis also differentiated itself from popular analytic theory in that it worked for a cure, rather than just an understanding of a person's pathology. TA understands that the early decisions we make are not immutable; we have choices and we can learn to think and believe differently.

The beliefs we learned, the concepts we decided on as a young child, happened with limited understanding and limited information, and can be modified, reconstructed or eliminated. We can make powerful new decisions as adults that literally change the course of our lives. And, unlike childhood, when these decisions were relatively unconscious, adulthood allows us to consciously engage in our decision-making process. We truly can change our life.

Transactional analysts further concluded that by the time people have grown into adults, they have developed a complete and comprehensive set of behavior patterns designed to prove or reinforce these early decisions. My clients, in the past 25 years, have convinced me that these conclusions are correct. The problem for children is that they make these decisions before their neural pathways and cognitive abilities are fully developed. It is with limited information and understanding that children decide things such as: "I'm bad," "I'm stupid," "I'm a burden," "I shouldn't be here," "It's all up to me," "I'm all alone," "I can't be me." Although these early decisions help children cope with their world at the time, they often become roadblocks later on.

In Summary

As young children, we operated from a set of genetic pre-dispositions, and what we lived through in our environments either enhanced or diminished them. We experienced relationships and began to make decisions about the way our relationships would be. These decisions were based on our early interactions with our parents and caregivers. They resulted in a set of core beliefs about ourselves, about others and about the way our lives would be, from which each of us operates. These core beliefs were imprinted in our brains as part of our conditioned chemistry.

Further, abusive situations and sensory deprivation such as neglect might have caused neurological programming that resulted in addictive or destructive relationships patterns as an adult. We do not escape our early conditioned chemistry. We re-create what we see over and over.

Transactional Analysis supports these ideas and works to help the individual permanently change beliefs that don't serve them in adulthood. These core beliefs, although imprinted in the brain, can be altered or replaced. In order to do this we must illuminate our early environmental conditions and determine the existential decisions we made as young children that no longer serve us.

Chapter Four

The Birth of Chemical Attraction

"Living a life is like constructing a building:
If you start wrong, you'll end wrong."
— Maya Angelou

I agree with Maya Angelou, except I would add, "Unless you go in and shore up the foundation." How we start our lives is, in essence, the determiner of how our lives will go. If we start out with relationships in which we are loved, secure and nurtured, we will develop thinking that supports happy, healthy adult relationships. If we start without love, security and nurturing, we are likely to develop thinking that undermines happy, healthy adult relationships.

The inception of this troubled thinking or belief system is the focus of this chapter. I want to take a look at exactly what happens that creates the kind of conditioned chemistry that generates our problems — essentially, how our experiences become that conditioned chemistry that sabotages our adult interacting. In later chapters we will examine exactly how to "shore up the foundation."

When a client comes to see me, it is almost always because something important in their relationships isn't working and it has reached a place where it is costing them more than they are willing to pay. They are having trouble and it is causing them pain and discomfort at a level they can no longer tolerate. Furthermore, their efforts to change the problem — usually over a long period of time — have failed and they are not feeling good about themselves.

One of the first things I do is to help them build a framework of understanding by looking at the inception of how they gave birth to their core beliefs, which became their chemistry tattoo. This way they can see what is hindering them.

I want my clients to understand exactly how they became who they are, and why they made the choices that brought them to this place in life, namely, my office. I want them to quickly experience relief from the shame, fear and anger they feel for being unable to experience the kind of relationships they need. I want them to know they are not "weird, unimportant, stupid, crazy or unlovable," rather that they are just like all the rest of us. They have a chemistry tattoo.

None of us can change what we cannot see and understand. So the first course of action is to begin to unveil what the client's core beliefs really are, where they came from and how they are impacting their relationships.

In this section on the birth of chemical attraction, we will look at the primary developmental pattern of attachment, along with the decision-making process we have as young children. This requires that we consider the results of less-than-perfect parenting, even abusive parenting, and the adaptations children learn in response to it.

In order to understand how our sabotaging beliefs appear in our life as adults, we must have a clear understanding of what happened to us as children, including the relationships we had with those closest to us. I have included lots of examples of how these beliefs manifest in adult behavior patterns and I will conclude with some specifics from my own life.

Attachment and Development

Attachment is the deep and enduring connection established between children and their caregivers in the first few years of life. It is the child's first love relationship and you can observe it developing in the gazing between parent and child that goes on during the feeding process. What the children see and construe in their mother's or father's eyes is what they come to believe about themselves: essentially, "I'm wanted" or "I'm not wanted." This connection, this attachment, profoundly influences every component of the human condition — mind, body, emotions, relationships, resilience and values.

Attachment is something that children and parents create together in an ongoing, shared relationship. If an infant interprets the gaze that he sees in his mother's eyes as she feeds him as, "You're my precious child and I'm so glad you are here," he will feel valued and safe. If the look in her eyes has absence of meaning, uncertainty and apprehension develops in the child. When there is negative meaning, God forbid, the child has no permission to be alive.

Children who fail to attach or bond emotionally to their parents grow up with low self-esteem, dependency issues and a lot of repressed anger that spills over into their relationships, making them stormy and intense. Their rigidity, hostility and dependency can push people away, which is the exact opposite of the connection that they desperately want and need.

Sometimes the child will emotionally attach to the father, an older sibling or grandparent, but failure to attach to the birthing parent has severe implications in the emotional life of a human being. Some of my women friends exclaim, "Not fair, this puts too much responsibility upon the woman." Fair or not, it appears to be true. It is incumbent upon our societies, then, to make adjustments for extended family leave for mothers with young children or make arrangements for onsite child care so that the mothers have frequent access to their child. This subject raises all sorts of sociological issues that cannot be addressed here, perhaps in a later work.

As infants, the healthy attachments we form are critical for our ability to grow into healthy adults and form satisfying relationships. Attachment is our first and most important developmental task and lays the foundation from which all further progress is made. In order for this attachment to take place, we needed to have a safe, secure, loving environment in which to bond with our caregivers. Without this, as we grow physically, we lack the emotional equipment to tackle our ensuing developmental tasks.

There are a number of these basic developmental tasks that children need to accomplish in order to become successfully functioning adults.

1. They need to explore their environment with feelings of safety and security, which leads to healthy cognitive and social development. We've all seen babies leave their mother's or father's presence in small steps, at first clinging to a parent's clothing. Then, cautiously, they let go, but they are looking back the whole time, checking in with their base, their center, their core of trust.

2. They need to learn basic trust and mutual exchange, which form a pattern for all future emotional relationships. They need to know they will be fed, changed and attended to on a regular basis. They need to be able to trust that their needs will be met.

3. They need to establish a moral framework, which involves developing empathy, compassion and conscience.

4. They need to develop the ability to self-soothe and self-regulate, in order to effectively manage their emotions and impulses.

5. They need to create a foundation for a sense of self, their own identity and a sense of competency, which builds self-worth, and the child needs to be guided into striking a balance between dependence and autonomy.

6. They need to generate the core belief systems that will serve them as adults, which consist of cognitive appraisals of, and decisions about, self, caregivers, others and life in general.

None of these developmental tasks can be firmly established without a secure attachment to a primary caregiver. Attachment to a caregiver who provides guidance and support is a basic human need, embedded in millions of years of evolution. We are born with an instinct to attach. Babies instinctively reach out for the safety and security of caregivers, and parents instinctively protect and nurture their offspring.

Children who begin their lives with the essential foundation of secure attachment fare better in all aspects of functioning as their development unfolds. Numerous longitudinal studies have demonstrated that securely attached infants and toddlers do better over time in the following areas:

- Self-esteem
- Independence and autonomy
- Resilience in the face of adversity
- Ability to manage impulses and feelings
- Long-term friendships
- Relationships with parents, caregivers and other authority figures
- Pro-social coping skills
- Trust, intimacy and affection
- Positive and hopeful belief systems about self, family and society
- Empathy, compassion and conscience
- Behavioral performance
- Academic success in school and corresponding success in careers
- Promote secure attachment in their own children when they become adults

Disrupted and anxious attachment not only leads to emotional and social problems, but also results in detrimental biochemical consequences in the developing brain. Children who are raised without loving touch and a sense of safety and security have abnormally high levels of stress hormones, which can impair the growth and development of their brains and bodies. The neurobiological consequences of emotional neglect can leave children disordered, depressed, apathetic, slow to learn, and prone to chronic mental and physical illness and drug addiction.

Children who begin their lives with compromised and disrupted attachment are at risk for serious problems as their development unfolds, such as:

- Low self-esteem
- Needy, clingy or pseudo-independent behaviors
- De-compensation when faced with stress and adversity
- Lack of self-control
- Maladaptive mental illness
- Clinical depression and anxiety
- Attention Deficit Disorder
- The inability to develop and maintain friendships
- Alienation from, or oppositional towards, parents, caregivers and other authority figures
- Antisocial attitudes and behaviors
- Aggression and violence
- Difficulty with genuine trust, intimacy and affection
- Negative, hopeless and pessimistic views of self, family and society
- A lack of empathy, compassion and remorse
- Behavioral and academic problems at school
- Problems at work
- A tendency to perpetuate the cycle of maltreatment and lack of attachment with their own children

The following is a basic understanding of secure versus compromised attachment in terms of how the individual views themselves, their caregivers and life in general. These varying states of attachment create the conditioned chemistry that dominates adult behavior patterns.

SECURE ATTACHMENT:

- **Of their self, the child decides:** "I am wanted, good, worthwhile, competent, important and lovable."
- **About their caregivers, they think:** "They are properly responsive to my needs, dependable, caring. I can trust them."
- **And of their life in the future:** "My world feels safe; life is good and worth living."

COMPROMISED ATTACHMENT:

- **About their self:** "I am unwanted, bad, stupid, a burden, not good enough, undeserving, not important, helpless, unlovable or worthless."
- **About their caregivers:** "They are unresponsive to my needs, insensitive, abusive, hurtful and untrustworthy. I can't trust them, can't depend upon them."
- **And about the way their life is and will be:** "My world feels scary and unsafe; life is hard, painful, hopeless and burdensome, perhaps even not worth living."

These secure versus compromised ways of looking at the world start forming at a pre-conscious level and are the basis for the conditioned chemistry forming our core beliefs. The young child that has not properly attached to its primary caretaker begins to think the world is unsafe, hard and painful, and creates a belief system based on those understandings. Then, as the child develops, they engage in a decision-making process about events and relationships in their world that is based on the emotional foundation associated with compromised attachment that creates their chemistry tattoo. They engage in roles and patterns of behavior based on those core understandings, and support them through a repetitive decision-making process designed to reinforce their primary beliefs about safety, security and love. One of the greatest human needs is to be able to trust our thinking, so our brain works to make us become experts at proving what it believes.

Following is a personal example. One of my core beliefs was, "I'm hurt and all alone." After I had spent some time in therapy I became able to see how I would set myself up to prove that belief. Once, after returning from a therapy workshop, I was tired and my husband happened to be in a bad mood. We got involved in an argument and I sanctimoniously told him he didn't have good coping skills. Infuriated, he called me a bad name and went off to sleep in the guest bedroom, leaving me "hurt and all alone!" Later in the night, the realization of how I had just created that scene hit me like a bolt of lightning. I went downstairs and apologized for my role in the problem.

The Decision-making Process

All children make decisions about the world and about how they must behave in order to survive, based on their early experiences. Depending on the level of attachment formed in early infancy, they are neurochemically predisposed to respond to their environments in different ways. Does the child feel safe, secure and loved? If yes, then they will engage in relationships and make decisions based on this safety. If not, then they will take on roles and behaviors to help them feel more safe and secure.

The child that was able to form a healthy attachment will encounter new people and new situations, and make the decision that it is safe to form relationships, safe to bond and safe to engage in healthy intimacy when grown. These individuals can more readily navigate school, work and their larger community, as their decision-making process is founded on positive ideas about the world. They can trust, and are open to the situations and opportunities that present themselves in their lives.

In contrast, the child from a compromised situation, where attachment has not occurred, where there is tension in the family, even abuse, can develop conditioned chemistry that causes them to become hyper-vigilant and decide they must take charge and control situations in order to be safe. The common denominator underlying *how* they take charge is that they must participate in role reversal and put the wants and needs of the parents, and eventually partners, friends and authority figures, above their own. These children develop a heightened sense of intuition in their effort to avoid turbulence.

I tell my clients that it's as if those children develop sensory antennae to scan their world and adapt to it to avoid being harmed. Some survive by making a decision to anticipate the needs of the adults or caregivers around them and working to meet those needs. Their decision-making process makes them pleasers and placaters. Their core belief might become, "I can't be me," and they may struggle with their own sense of identity as adults.

Other children will decide to work very hard, taking care of the household chores, looking after the younger children and trying to follow the sometimes-unpredictable rules in order to avoid the mayhem. They become the "bossy little staff sergeants," commanding and directing everything and everyone around them. Such a child might hold the core belief, "It's all up to me." That child might think, "If I work hard enough and get enough done, maybe things will be okay."

Still others become "the clown:" teasing, making light of, minimizing and trying desperately to re-direct the tension. Sometimes one child becomes the scapegoat, the angry delinquent, engaging in scandalous behavior that brings unwanted attention to the family. They act out a desperate cry: "Can't anyone see that something is terribly wrong here?"

Then there is the lost child, the one who simply withdraws into his or her own world. They make a decision not to connect with anyone or anything. They simply avoid the insanity by making themselves absent.

Everyone has both positive and negative occurrences going on in their environment. Almost no one makes entirely negative decisions about themselves. There are usually some positive decisions to counteract the negative ones; otherwise, we would never succeed at anything.

Whatever kind of decision-making process a child engages in, they respond to their environment by doing the best they can, given their circumstances. In compromised situations the decision-making process often creates roles for children that put them in adult-like positions where they are robbed of their rightful childhoods: safe, secure childhoods of exploration, play and self-development.

Parenting

The kind of parenting we received as children makes an enormous difference in who we become as adults. If our parents were loving and predictable, fostering that necessary attachment, we have one kind of experience. If they were cold, unpredictable or abusive and did not work towards adequate attachment, we had a very different kind of experience.

Many of us experienced some form of compromised parenting during our childhood in the form of emotionally-unavailable caregivers, unpredictability, lack of safety, yelling or other forms of emotional abuse, inadequate physical care, or even physical and sexual abuse. These compromised circumstances result in experiences that generate conditioned chemistry that forms core beliefs about the world, and these core beliefs then impact the way we interact with our larger environment.

Most parents, even the most patient ones, lose their temper and yell at their children from time to time. While occasional yelling is common in American families, parents who constantly yell at their children are subjecting their children to emotional abuse that researchers say can be as harmful as physical abuse. Yelling and other forms of emotional abuse can be a more significant predictor of mental illness than sexual or physical abuse.

Parents naturally want their children to behave in certain ways and not to behave in other ways, and they give their children instructions accordingly: "Have these attributes," or, in other words, "Be this way." And injunctions are given: "Don't be this way." When these attributions and injunctions (which will be discussed in greater detail later on) are enforced too harshly and too often — with a driven nature about them — it can cause the child to think something like, "If I don't, I'm not okay," causing children to make negative decisions about themselves. They begin, out of their awareness, to develop what Transactional Analysts (TAs) call driver behaviors: actions that seem to have a driven nature about them. I'm going to utilize some of the TA terminology here because I think it helps people understand themselves better than the clinical jargon of psychology or psychiatry.

Dr. Eric Berne, the founder of TA, believed that for every attribution given to a child, there is an unspoken injunction. For example,

- "Be strong" could also mean, "Don't feel."
- "Be perfect" can mean, "Don't fail, don't make mistakes."
- "Please me" could also mean, "Don't be you, don't have needs."
- "Be careful" can be interpreted as, "Be scared, don't trust."
- "Hurry up" can mean, "Don't relax."
- "Work hard" can be turned into, "Don't play, don't rest."

When we work hard to please others so that we can be accepted or included, we can lose touch with our own feelings and needs. Worse, we can lose our sense of identity. Our authentic self can become buried somewhere inside, taking a back seat to everyone else. And when we do that, we eventually become sad, hurt and angry ... mostly at ourselves. When we ignore who we really are for too long, that buried part of our personality will sometimes become active and use a number of methods to get our attention ... acting out behaviors that are unlike us. Or we will develop anxiety, depression and other illnesses ... all designed by our inner self in an attempt to get our attention and address our buried needs.

Children who have to work too hard, particularly at an early age, feel guilty when they try to rest or relax, as adults. They developed conditioned chemistry for "doing" rather than "being" and they can make work out of any activity, including vacation. The injunction for work hard is, "Don't rest; don't relax."

Children who are ignored or told to be strong — especially when they are lonely, sad, scared or hurt — learn to disconnect from their feelings; as adults, they have trouble with intimacy and spontaneity. Their partners and children come into my office complaining that they're too unemotional and no fun.

When we grow up with the message that we are or should be perfect, we develop enormous anxiety and sometimes become obsessive about details. This obsessive behavior compensates for our fear of missing something or making a mistake. We have high expectations and a high fear of failure that apply to others and ourselves. It is exhausting for us and for everyone around us.

Children who grow up in an atmosphere where they are programmed to be nice, please everyone and keep the peace, have difficulty defining clearly who they are, what they think and especially how they feel. They have trouble knowing what they want and making long-term plans. When they do identify what they want and make long-term plans, they have trouble feeling passionate and aggressively pursuing their dream. They complain about their partners always having their way, but if the partner says, "Where would you like to go for dinner," they say, "I don't know, you decide."

All of us can benefit from some form of training in these attributions. Life can be difficult and sometimes we need to be strong. It is important to exercise caution and not be too impulsive when making decisions, so that we don't act too hastily and regret it later. Working hard and pleasing others can be a rewarding and fulfilling experience. The problem arises when we are driven to do these things in order to feel okay, to feel loved, to feel valuable and be accepted. It is then that the dysfunction occurs.

Whatever style of caregiving our particular parents engaged in, we formed our core beliefs, our conditioned chemistry, based on it. If those core beliefs are no longer serving us as adults, it is time to make a change. I tell my clients that we honor our parents, not by living out their foibles, nor by blaming them for our problems, but by taking responsibility to keep what they taught us that works well for us and discard what doesn't.

Adaptations

All children, and particularly those who have suffered any kind of compromised parental interactions, develop characteristics or assume roles in response to the early beliefs they have formed. How pronounced these roles become depends upon three critical elements: the strength and integrity of the healthier parent (if there was one), the individual genetic mapping and the cultural/environmental experience. These combine to give the child a certain amount of resilience, ability to profit from their experience and, most importantly, the ability to change. Adaptation, after all, has been the hallmark of our survival since the beginning of time.

Adaptive behaviors are learned. Children are powerless over their lives and must learn how to survive within the environment in which they are born. They must adapt. As I stated in an earlier chapter, soon after birth children begin trying to figure out who they are, who the people around them are and what is going on in their environment. Then they must figure out what they have to do and whom they have to be in order to survive.

This figuring out process elicits the child's adaptive abilities as they work to effectively function in everyday life and meet familial, social and community expectations. Infants learn to roll over, to crawl and eventually to walk. Older children learn to dress themselves, to brush their teeth and to talk. They learn to follow a great variety of rules while interacting with other people, such as when to say excuse me, please and thank you.

Good adaptive behavior can develop in children when their basic needs are being met on a consistent basis and when they are not subjected to neglect, deprivation or abuse. When children are able to develop healthy, adaptive behaviors, they are more independent at home, more successful in their interpersonal relationships, and more successful at school and out in the community.

Conversely, when children's needs are not being met, when they are exposed to neglect or abuse, their adaptive responses can result in undesirable or socially inappropriate behaviors. Just as a child can develop difficulties in mastering basic functional skills, such as walking, talking or toileting, maladaptive behaviors can interfere with the acquisition of desired interpersonal and social skills, causing both learning and social problems. These maladaptive behavior patterns can occur in children of any age and from any cultural background or socioeconomic level, but they always occur at higher levels in children of neglect and abuse.

The kind of adaptive behaviors that an individual develops is specific to his/her given environment, and can be prolonged for generations through role modeling that becomes conditioned chemistry. What we become accustomed to, become familiar with, is what we gravitate towards as adults, whether it's good for us or not.

A young boy who comes from an environment with a controlling mother and a passive father might adapt by acquiescing to his mother's control and modeling his behavior after his father. He then generalizes this adaptive behavior to the larger social world by submitting to the wishes and needs of others over his own. He may marry a controlling partner and model his maladaptive behavior to his own children, perpetuating the pattern.

Personally, I grew up with a verbally and physically abusive father and a weak, passive mother who was helpless to deal with him. I adapted by playing the role of mother — arguing and standing up to my father and trying to protect my younger siblings from his wrath. This adaptive behavior, co-mingled with my core belief, "It's all up to me," created conditioned chemistry that led me to engage in relationships where I was in charge and dominant. Ironically, that was the last thing I needed. I needed a partner strong enough to assume an equal part of the responsibility in a relationship.

Temperament

The way a child adapts, in part, relates to its temperament. If you have a naturally extroverted child and a quiet, introverted mother, the mother may force the child to become a quiet person, reinforcing quiet behaviors. Since this is not the child's true nature, the child's response in trying to please his or her mother is maladaptive. Assuming a role of the quiet child will have repercussions to their sense of self down the road, as they often feel, "I can't be me." One of the things I hear from their partners is, "I'm not sure who he/she is."

If you have a messy, creative, sanguine child and the mother or caregiver is obsessive about structure and order, the child may take on adaptive behaviors that aim to please. However, Mom's complaints, criticisms and comparisons may cause the child to feel not good enough, as they continually try to be something they are not. This adaptive behavior can continue into adulthood. These individuals will have difficulty following through because their adaptive behavior has reinforced a belief that whatever they do won't be good enough, so why bother. Their partner complains that they never finish or follow through with things.

Conditioned Chemistry in Adulthood

What kind of mother, father, husband, wife, friend, neighbor or employee does a child grow up to be? It depends upon the role they assumed in connection with their core beliefs. If their early decisions were primarily positive, they can grow up to be fairly well balanced individuals in any role they choose. But if their beliefs were based upon an unhealthy parental relationship — where chaos and intense emotions reigned — their adaptive behaviors and core beliefs may cause them to experience significant difficulty maintaining a healthy balance in their adult relationships.

There are numerous roles that individuals carry forward from childhood into their adult relationships. Some are staff sergeants: serious, perfectionistic, rigid and intense. They may have decided, "It's all up to me" and their adaptive behavior pattern is to take charge and work hard. They lack a sense of humor, so those in relationships with them find themselves enmeshed in an intense, stormy melodrama, which is extremely difficult to live with.

Some individuals become the super achieving, super responsible hero, who nobody can live up to. Or they become the scapegoat. Angry, paranoid and isolated, their spouses/partners end up living in a malaise, feeling depressed, lonely and used up.

Then there is the clown, whose primary behavior patterns are focused on pleasing others and their core belief likely is, "I can't be me." These individuals do everything they can to keep everybody else happy. They will go to great lengths to keep the peace because they have an aversion to confrontation. They are also unable to accept much responsibility and are excessively oriented towards pleasure and leisure. Their children and partners can feel like parents because the clown won't focus on anything serious or take charge of anything.

All of us have formed core beliefs as children that set us up to act in certain ways as adults. These core beliefs, over time, become tattooed into conditioned chemistry in our brain. No doubt most of us made both positive and negative decisions about ourselves. Without some positive beliefs we would never achieve anything. However, we are focusing here on some of the more negative decisions children make about themselves, the decisions that become problematic in adulthood and become the conditioned chemistry we need to overcome. These decisions can hinder one's progress by resulting in unhealthy behavior patterns. The following is a synopsis of some of the most common negative beliefs we birthed as children, and some of the accompanying behavior patterns we might experience as adults.

Negative Core Beliefs

"I'm not good enough." These individuals usually settle for less than what they might have and achieve less than they are able. Even if they create a successful situation where they excel, they often sabotage any gains by failing to finish projects or by surrendering their leadership to someone else. They need constant reassurance and often lean on their inferiors. Ultra-sensitive to criticism, even the slightest disagreement or disapproval can raise high levels of anxiety, as the smallest mistake can trigger the fear of inadequacy. Their partners tell me that they often walk on eggs to avoid hurting their feelings. And, at some point, partners become really tired of doing that and start saying, "Don't be so sensitive."

"It's all up to me." This individual won't ask for help, stays overworked and takes charge of people and events, sometimes inappropriately. Others experience them as bossy or too controlling. Because they don't ask for help, they develop family and social relationships with people who are needy or narcissistic, people who want to be helped (served). Chronic fatigue is familiar to this person. When this person is finally able to express a need

— usually when they are exhausted or sick — their milieu is either unaware or unconcerned because their relationships are based on one-sided giving.

"I don't count, I don't matter." These individuals are usually passive and submissive. Unable to say no or express disagreement, their anger is rarely seen and when it is, it is passive aggressive … undercover. Always giving in to others, they end up resenting those to whom they submit. They have low self-esteem, low energy and sometimes isolate themselves. They tend to choose friends or partners who are either handicapped or beneath them socially or economically.

"My needs don't matter." Often pleasing everyone else and not taking care of themselves, these individuals don't always know what their needs are. Sometimes they are so unaware, they end up leaving themselves neglected or unprotected, or worse, tolerating abuse. They are pleasers, peacemakers and, sometimes, patsies. They are in danger of marrying partners who are too controlling or too self-absorbed.

"I'm hurt." These individuals are comfort seekers. They look for people to take care of them and remain immature about certain issues, like managing money or taking care of the house. Oblivious and distractible, they sometimes lack awareness of their immediate surroundings and are accident-prone. This person expects bad things to happen. They are overly sensitive and easily hurt by the slightest criticism. In fact, they read bad intentions into even the mildest mishap and expect the outcome to be harmful. Partners of this type of individual often tell me that they feel like this person is a child rather than an adult.

"I'm scared." Hyper-vigilant, they often have stomach problems, elimination issues, panic attacks and respiratory problems; they sometimes grind their teeth. Anxious and tense, they don't like surprises and are not flexible. They don't adjust to changes in plans or schedule, and tend to resist or pout when forced to adapt.

"I'm sad." These individuals have a flat affect and little to no facial expression when speaking. They often speak in a monotone, the volume drifting off at the end of their sentences. With chronic depression and low energy, this person often shows a lack of initiative and never seems happy or joyful about anything; nothing makes them happy. They experience multiple somatic aches and pains.

"I'm a burden." These individuals have significant trouble being alone and, in times of high stress, will have suicidal ideation. Identity and self-worth are critical issues; they tend to adapt to the identity of those with whom they are in a relationship, always deferring to that person in terms of wants and needs. They look for someone who will take care of them. They are apologizing, anxious, depressed and, sometimes, very, very angry.

"My life is hard." People of this belief carry the weight of the world on their shoulders. They are slightly stooped, chronically fatigued and appear to have a black cloud hanging over them. They constantly talk about how hard is to make money, how hard it is to meet people, how hard their marriage is, how their life is hard. In relationships, they are dependent. They need someone stronger to lean on, someone who can make their life easier.

"I'm angry." Usually cold, unfeeling or indifferent, with stormy, intense relationships, these individuals are quick to criticize or complain. They look for what's bad in others or wrong in any situation so they can vent their anger. Focused on injustice, life has dealt them a raw deal and it isn't fair. Blaming others for their troubles and their lot in life, they tend to stay detached in relationships, and often end up isolated and lonely.

"I can't trust." These people rarely feel safe, in relationships or in life. They look for evidence of betrayal and often choose partners who cheat. Their partners are always on trial and walking on eggs to avoid giving the slightest impression of unfaithfulness. Hyper-vigilant, these people try to micromanage everyone and everything around them.

"I'll never get what I want" or "I'll never be happy." Chronically dissatisfied people, they experience an ever-present sense of emptiness and loneliness. Nothing is ever enough to change their overall outlook. Lots of apathy and joylessness; nothing makes them happy. They tend to whine and engage in daydreaming and wishful thinking. "If only" is one of their frequent expressions.

"I'm worthless." A state of misery best describes the daily experience of these people. Dejected, they feel hopeless that anything will ever improve for them. They live in a world of melancholy, where chronic depression and apathy reign. Suicidal thoughts are a regular visitor to their brain. They have low energy, lots of self-hate and are experts at creating self-defeating patterns of behavior. Their partners come to see me exhausted, because nothing they can do or say makes these people feel better.

"I'm stupid." These individuals do poorly in school and in life. Lacking self-confidence, they cannot trust their own judgment. They allow others to define them and run their lives.

"I'm crazy." Unable to trust themselves or anyone else, they live in a constant state of fear. They cannot trust their own judgment so they look for someone else who will think for them. Confusion and indecisiveness best describe their state of mind. Panic attacks are common, as they have an intense fear of their surroundings.

"I'm all alone." This person doesn't trust anyone. Their relationships with their early caregivers were unpredictable or unreliable or both. Although they are lonely and need connection, they are uncomfortable with emotional intimacy and are afraid to become close to anyone. When someone begins to get too close, they push him or her away. They don't ask for help, even in difficult circumstances. "I'll do it myself" is a much-used phrase. Very uncomfortable in a crowd and sometimes reclusive, these people are loners.

"I can't be me." These people lose touch with their true selves. They become a chameleon, thinking, "I have to be whatever they want me to be." They have identity problems because they shut down their feelings and needs long ago. Their friends and family often complain about how often they change and wonder who they really are. When asked what they think or want, they will tell you what you think or want. They experience chronic low-grade depression and over a long period of time may become filled with despair and bitterness.

"I'm bad." These people show a lot of shame in their body language, won't meet your eyes for very long, can't accept a compliment and fidget uncomfortably when singled out for attention. They have trouble being alone; only when someone else is around can they escape that horrible thought. Usually, they operate well beneath their capability and sometimes turn to crime or antisocial behaviors. Often, they choose other "bad" people as their social group. Vulnerable to substance abuse, they need to numb themselves from their painful reality.

"I shouldn't be." This is the most clinically significant of all negative beliefs a person can have. It is often found in those who commit suicide. These people isolate, have chronic depression, don't connect with or commit to anyone, and make no long-term plans. They have difficulty maintaining interest in anything, and have low energy and lots of apathy. This person has no permission to live, so everything they do is hard.

The vast majority of us have one or more of these negative self-beliefs. The extent to which the belief controls our life depends upon how severe, constant and chronic the environment was in which the belief was generated.

Since the ability to trust our own thinking is a critical human need, the early decisions we make about ourselves and others cause us to establish patterns of behavior for the purpose of proving what we believe. These behavior patterns significantly impact, and to a considerable extent control, the way we live … how well we do in school, with whom we choose to be in relationships, the success and failures of those relationships, the choices about our careers, and our lives in general.

My Life

The following information gives you a glimpse of what was happening in my childhood that led me to develop the core beliefs that I had. Some of my beliefs were positive and helped me to get an education and develop a comfortable lifestyle, while others created roadblocks, sometimes landslides.

From my father and paternal grandmother, I experienced preferential treatment and positive expectations. I often spent the night with my Grandmother Laura, who taught me music and told me I was smart and pretty. One summer, with the help of a seamstress, she made me a beautiful white lace dress trimmed in blue ribbon and bought me blue shoes to match. In the winter, when I stayed with her, she would put me in my favorite bedroom, iron the sheets and wrap me in her own flannel gowns to make sure I was toasty warm. She kept me constantly at her side when I visited and would teach me what she was doing … playing her pump organ (I would sing and turn the pages of the music), baking bread for the farmhands, or crocheting doilies to place under her kerosene lamps.

My daddy also favored me, sometimes buying me pretty dresses or shoes, or taking me to work with him when he was building houses. I got to hold the nails for him. At home, when food was scarce, he sometimes made sure that he and I had eggs or meat when no one else did. My daddy bragged about how strong and smart I was, and told me I could be anything I wanted to be.

The positive decisions I made, which helped me to become successful later in life, were based on what I heard from the important people in my life on a recurring basis. In addition to my father and his mother, other family members, schoolteachers, church members and friends told me that I was smart, pretty and such a good singer that I should sing for the Grand Ole Opry.

My first grade teacher, Miss Mary Brown, took a great liking to me, made me clothes, had me sing at school events and told me I'd be successful someday. I heard those things over and over from enough people that I came to believe them, and so I decided, "I'm smart and pretty and I'm important. I should have what I want. I can be successful. I'm talented and likeable; people will help me. I'm strong; I can make it if I work hard and don't give up."

On the other hand, I made many negative decisions and developed negative core beliefs that drove my conditioned chemistry. These negative beliefs were based on the deprivation, neglect and abuse I experienced from both my parents and in my environment.

Life at home was crowded and chaotic, often violent and always unpredictable. My father was out of work and drunk much of the time. He would beat one of the kids on a regular basis, whether he was drunk or not. My mother was usually pregnant and unhappy. She was afraid of everything and needed the children home with her. She depended upon me to help her clean the house and care for the younger children. When I wanted time to myself, she called me selfish and accused me of not caring about her or my siblings. I felt angry and embarrassed by the dire conditions in which we lived: dirt floors, no screens on the doors or windows and no indoor plumbing.

We sometimes went for days without food. Weeks would pass when we ate nothing but biscuits and white flour gravy made with grease, flour and water — no protein. The only nutrients we got were whatever was in the white flour.

I was very much aware of my anger and disappointment, but I had no idea how wounded and impaired I would become because of my parents' neglect and abuse. I felt alone and thought everything at home was up to me. Mother couldn't stand up to my dad and I was the one trying to get him to stop the beatings. He didn't beat me until the day I ran away, but if I didn't please him, he verbally abused me and ignored me. They also left me alone to take care of my younger siblings when I was far too young. It started to become clear to me that in order to avoid their wrath, it was my job to please them and meet their needs.

After I left home, I lived with a number of other families. Living in the homes of strangers, I worked hard and walked on eggshells, being careful not to make anyone angry, saying yes when I wanted to say no, not really being myself, but rather trying to be what they needed me to be. I decided I had to please them because not knowing how long I would have a place to stay, a bed to sleep in or food to eat was a terrifying experience. So I tried very hard to please people, hoping to fit in and hoping they would keep me. I was easily hurt by others at the slightest rebuff and became an expert at withdrawing into aloneness — into my dreams about another life, a life where I would be safe and secure.

The following are the negative core beliefs that I developed as a result of what I was experiencing in my early years. I find it fascinating that the decisions we make about our lives very early can be further solidified by additional experiences. That certainly happened to me while I was living in the homes of strangers. My early beliefs were reinforced, including: "I'm hurt and I'm all alone. It's all up to me. I can't trust anyone. I can't be me, I have to please them. But, if I can be what they want, do everything right, please everyone and take care of their needs, maybe they'll love/keep/help me. If I work hard and run fast, I can make it for a while."

When we make these early decisions, they are cumulative and begin to connect, forming a picture in a child's mind that says, "This is who I have to be to make it and this is the way my life is going to be," thus forming the core beliefs from which we operate throughout our lives. I have found myself sometimes operating from these core beliefs, even after I became trained as a therapist and had been in practice for a number of years. Change is a process; it takes time to change what we gave birth to as our fundamental ways of thinking.

In Summary

This chapter was designed to look at the inception of conditioned chemistry, which is based on our early cognitive decisions. The processes of bonding with our initial caregivers and responding to our environments are complicated ones that are nuanced for each individual. And they established conditioned chemistry that plays a significant role in who we choose as a partner.

There are no givens. Some children fare better, even with abuse, because of the genetic traits with which they were born. Some children from compromised beginnings have relatives and mentors who help offset early conditioning as they grow. Some children come from dysfunctional homes with alcohol or drug abuse and are neglected, but are greatly loved.

Every individual has a unique story that brought them to where they are as adults. Becoming aware and accepting of this story is what starts the healing process. Bringing those early decisions to consciousness and changing what doesn't work allows us to truly become ourselves, who we were really meant to be. Then, when we have completed that process, we are able to make healthy choices about our relationships.

Chapter Five

Understanding Your Conditioned Chemistry

*"The outer conditions of a person's life will always
be found to reflect their inner beliefs."*
— *James Allen*

When you become aware that certain aspects of your life are not working and that the difficulty lies inside you, not necessarily with the other person, then you are ready to make changes. If you can accept the premise that your inner world is creating your outer world, you can begin to address the source of your difficulties. This is the first step towards any significant relationship transformation.

When you are able to move beyond your defenses and denial, and look openly and honestly inside, you can clearly see what you need to change. You can't change what you can't see and you won't change what you don't own as your "stuff." You must identify your negative core beliefs, understand them, and then you can make a conscious choice to let them go and replace them with new beliefs.

The first stage in this process is to identify your negative core beliefs and become thoroughly familiar with them. You might ask, "Why would I want to become familiar with them when they have caused me so much trouble?" Because there was a time in your life when those beliefs may have served you well, or at least served to protect you in some way. The part of you that originally embraced those beliefs won't let go of them easily, and you will need to lovingly (not critically) take control and convince your child self that these beliefs are no longer helpful and that you can change.

This chapter is intended to look in-depth at exactly how to accomplish getting to know your conditioned chemistry, accepting your negative core beliefs and letting them go. I have included sections that address the awareness of your core beliefs and the acceptance and letting go/healing of them. These sections give you an understanding of the tools I use in my practice and will help you successfully maneuver through this process.

In utilizing these tools you will engage in some self-reflection, and you may want to put pen to paper and record your thoughts for better clarity. Journaling your process allows you to review the work you are doing. Reviewing is valuable, as it strengthens your brain's neural pathways and reinforces the new chemistry you are trying to create.

Starting at the beginning, I will help you move through different exercises that will reveal your negative core beliefs, help you make peace with them and move on without them. These exercises are brief and to the point; they unfold in a simple and systematic way.

Awareness

Being fully aware is critical to your success, and it takes diligence. Most people begin this process by reaching a point of wanting to make change and they want this change enough that they are willing to move out of their comfort zone to create it. Something in their lives is not working and they recognize the need to understand what it is, to become aware.

If you repeatedly experience negative results, you do have core beliefs operating that have become troublemakers, a form of unwanted conditioned chemistry. You have to be aware of what you believe and what thinking underlies your behavior before you can change it. These troublemaking core beliefs that are creating restrictive, self-limiting or even self-destructive outcomes are usually completely unconscious. And because they are so often unconscious, it is easy to continually allow them to dictate your behavior, no matter how much you wish they didn't.

These unconscious and potentially destructive behavior patterns can chip away at your self-esteem as you continually engage in behaviors that generate unpleasant results. You may eat too much and stay overweight, struggle with exercise and feel sluggish, stay underemployed and lack enough money, or you may remain in unfulfilling relationships that undermine your happiness. Destructive behavior patterns can manifest in a variety of ways, but what they all have in common are core belief systems that maintain the behaviors.

The beliefs that underlie these behaviors are your personal conditioned chemistry and their corresponding behaviors can make you feel stupid or even crazy. You may have tried to change, but no matter how often you try to get different results, this conditioned chemistry can keep you perpetually acting from your self-destructive patterns of behavior. You fail to make lasting change in your relationships, fail to get the results you want, and once again you end up feeling helpless, even hopeless.

The only solution I know that works to create different results is to become fully aware of your conditioned chemistry and replace it. It is impossible to become someone different until we become aware of, and accept the reality of, who we are now. We cannot change what we continue to avoid. We must be willing to face the dark part of ourselves and become aware, for it is what we think we can't face that oppresses us the most.

I have developed tools to bring about this awareness that include an intake interview, questionnaires and exercises. They are all designed to look at what drives you (Attributions and Injunctions, in TA terminology). These tools build on one another, allowing you to get a clear idea and awareness of what your underlying core beliefs consist of.

Intake

I begin the intake process by having my clients ask themselves a series of questions. "What do I want? How did I get here? What brought me to this place in my life?" Next, I help them understand what their inherited traits and conditions are and to look at the early existential decisions they made about themselves and about their way life.

Most of us have thought about why things are not working in our lives and we have at least a vague idea of some of the limiting core beliefs we hold. You might think, "My father always said, 'Life is hard work,' and now it seems that everything I do is difficult. Why is it like that for me?" Although you might have an idea about your belief system if your father always reinforced that "life is hard work," your actual core beliefs are likely a combination of beliefs operating at an unconscious level that include: "Life is hard."

Fortunately or unfortunately, human nature has a tendency to "fight or flight" in response to unpleasant thoughts and experiences. This leaves most of us naturally suppressing our negative beliefs in an attempt to avoid pain. Avoiding pain is a healthy survival instinct, but it doesn't serve us when we need to clearly see what is in the way of our success. As a matter of fact, avoidance is one of the major stumbling blocks to personal growth.

As long as we remain unaware of our actual beliefs, we will continue to generate behavior patterns that net specific results based on beliefs like, "Life is hard." What we believe, we will create. In order to create a different outcome, we need to become aware.

EXERCISE I: STARTING POINT

Your initial awareness takes place by thinking about a series of questions. If you are interested in utilizing this tool while you read, I suggest you write down your answers and begin to form a picture of your beliefs. The questions are:

- What do you like about yourself?
- What do you dislike about yourself?
- What kind of person are you?
- What do you believe in?
- What is right in your life?
- What are you unhappy about?
- What are you most afraid of?
- What makes you feel angry, sad or hurt?

When responding to these questions, I find it can be difficult to readily answer deeply and honestly the first time. You may need to ponder these questions and contemplate your answers. I want you to do a fearless, comprehensive inventory of your innermost self. I want you to allow yourself enough time to know what you truly feel and believe. I want you to allow yourself to know what you are afraid of and face the things you can't say to others. Take a close look at what thoughts and feelings came up that you pushed back down.

If answering these questions generates a noticeable level of pain or discomfort, talk to someone you trust. Get support!

After you answer these initial questions, ask yourself one further question: "If you could wave a magic wand and change anything about yourself, what would you change?" This question needs to be given some thought. You must really look at what is important and what you want in your life, how you want to be. Do not allow yourself to limit your thinking to old patterns. We tend to focus on why we can't have, do, become what we want rather than exploring the possibilities. Remember, it's a magic wand; let yourself freely visualize what your life would be like if it was exactly as you wish.

With this information in place, you can next complete an exercise to look at the potentially inherited and/or learned beliefs that came from your caregivers or parents.

EXERCISE II: WHAT WE LEARNED/INHERITED FROM OUR PARENTS

I want you to think back to as early as you can remember and envision your parents or those who raised you. Make a list of the things you liked the best and the least about each primary caregiver. Use descriptive adjectives and language that a grade-school child could understand. Regarding my own parents, I wrote the following:

Liked about Dad:
- Intelligent
- Talented
- Handsome
- Entrepreneur
- Creative
- Hard Working (at times)

Liked about Mom:
- Pretty
- Caring
- Good Singer
- Talented
- Good Cook
- Hardworking (at times)

Disliked about Dad:
- Violent Temper
- Alcoholic
- Lazy
- Frivolous with Money/Resources
- Arrogant
- Self-Centered
- Verbally and Physically Abusive
- Unpredictable and Unreliable
- He Expected Me to be The Parent

Disliked about Mom:
- Undisciplined
- Anxious
- Food Addict
- Unassertive/Couldn't Say No
- Unpredictable and Unreliable
- Frivolous with Money/Resources
- She Expected Me to be The Parent

The first thing to note is where there is a double dose of role modeling. When you see traits duplicated under both parents, these are the traits you are more likely to have inherited and/or taken on. In my case, I am intelligent, talented, hardworking, caring, supportive and known for my creativity — all positive traits of my parents.

When I first entered therapy, I wanted to understand my difficulty in relationships, my lack of self-discipline and my inconsistent ability to stay focused. I couldn't find a partner, I was gaining weight and I made money but couldn't save any. I was anxious, a pleaser and found it difficult to say no to others. I also had some significant anger issues with men, although I rarely showed it.

As you can see, I developed traits that were the best and the worst of both parents. I developed certain negative core beliefs from my mother's fear and passivity, and from my father's aggression and verbal/emotional abuse. I also developed positive core beliefs related to my talent, my intelligence and my ability to work hard and succeed, which have served me well.

In completing this exercise, you may be surprised to find what characteristics you remember. This exercise, combined with the first intake questions, will form a base for identifying your core beliefs.

EXERCISE III: QUESTIONNAIRE

Next, we will examine who you are, how you got where you are and why you have the issues that you do. You are the product of your genetic mapping and your parental and cultural programming. You are also heavily influenced, sometimes controlled, by the existential decisions about yourself and others that you made as a young child in circumstances you didn't understand and couldn't control.

Please answer the following questions in relation to the people who raised you:

Mother/Mother Figure:
1. What was your mother's favorite saying about life?
2. How did your mother praise you? What did she say? What did she do?
3. How did your mother criticize you? What did she say? What did she do?
4. When your mother was upset, how did she show it? And how did you respond?
5. What was her advice to you as a child?

Father/Father Figure:
1. What was your father's favorite saying about life?
2. How did your father praise you? What did he say? What did he do?
3. How did your father criticize you? What did he say? What did he do?
4. When your father was upset, how did he show it? And what did you do to help?
5. What was his advice to you as a child?

In General:
1. When you were punished, what was mild and what was severe?
2. Which punishment was most common?

Please reflect and describe the following:
1. What feelings, thoughts or attitudes were you NOT to reveal in your childhood?
2. What do you now say and believe about life?

3. What did you say and believe about life as a teenager?

4. What do you like most about yourself?

5. What do you dislike about yourself?

6. If someone disagrees with you, do you generally argue or give in?

7. When you feel upset or uncomfortable, describe the feeling you most often have.

Out of these answers, you may begin to see some patterns that fit with the different core beliefs mentioned in Chapter 4. If you take the time to review these by reading through them very slowly, you are bound to resonate with certain ones. Make a brief list of the ones you resonate with. We will work with them again in Chapter 7. Here they are again in brief:

- "I'm not good enough."
- "It's all up to me."
- "I don't count, I don't matter."
- "My needs don't matter."
- "I'm hurt."
- "I'm scared."
- "I'm sad."
- "I'm a burden."
- "My life is hard."
- "I'm angry."
- "I can't trust anyone."
- "I'll never get what I want."
- "I'm worthless."
- "I'm stupid."
- "I'm crazy."
- "I'm all alone."
- "I can't be me."
- "I'm bad."
- "I shouldn't be."

Again, a more descriptive list can be found in Chapter 4. If you have identified a couple of likely candidates, you may want to go back and refresh yourself about some of the accompanying behavior patterns to see if they fit.

Attributions and Injunctions

Next it is important to understand the attributions and injunctions (verbal and nonverbal directives) we were receiving as children that caused us to develop our negative core beliefs. Becoming familiar with your conditioned chemistry, getting to know all the intricacies of how your negative core beliefs came into being, is primary. The more familiar you are with your beliefs and how you acquired them, the more you are in a position to change them.

Attributions and injunctions are the instructions you received from your primary caretakers about how to be, how to live in the world. Very early, our parents and caregivers started putting conditions on us, admonitions to be this way and don't be that way. In responding to these conditions, we began to understand that the world wanted us to act in certain ways and not in other ways.

For example, if your grandmother always said to you, "Put on a smile," you were getting a strong message (attribution) to please her. This message has another side to it (injunction), which says don't be yourself. These kinds of messages, when they were given to us regularly throughout our childhood, would have generated beliefs that required us to please others above ourselves and might have culminated in a core belief about ourselves like, "I can't be me" or "I don't matter." Nobody may have said this directly, but the attributions, combined with their injunctions, which you heard over and over, implied this message and generated that belief. Overall, the way we navigated what we were and weren't supposed to do or be as children is of major importance in better understanding our conditioned chemistry.

So, what were you expected to do and what were you expected not to do, as a child? How were you expected to be?

You can determine your programmed attributions (be like this) and your programmed injunctions (don't be like that) by looking at the messages you got as a child. Then you can identify the resulting core beliefs and behavior patterns that developed as a result of trying to accommodate the attributions and injunctions. Remember, for every attribution there is an injunction: Work hard can mean don't play, don't relax. When a parent says, "Buck up, you can take it …" the message is be strong. But be strong can also mean don't feel.

The most common childhood attributions and their injunctions are as follows:

Attributions (Be)	Injunctions (Don't Be)
Be Perfect	Don't Fail
Please Me	Don't Be You
Be Strong	Don't Feel, Don't Have Needs
Be Careful	Be Scared, Don't Take Risks
Work Hard	Don't Relax
Hurry Up	Don't Stop and Think

In reading this list you may again resonate with certain attributions and injunctions. Perhaps your mother was fearful and continually told you to be careful in various ways. "Don't touch that." "Wash your hands." "Look for cars when you cross the street." "Wear your helmet." "Wear your coat or you'll get sick." "Tie your shoes or you'll trip." They all translate into "Be careful!" Along with that attribution to be careful comes the injunction to be scared, don't take risks. This teaches a child to believe the world isn't safe and to operate from the understanding that they should be afraid. None of those statements standing alone would create a problem; the problem comes when they are repeated too many times and are accompanied by fearful body language.

Attributions and injunctions are closely tied to the development of core beliefs, and like core beliefs, they come in multiples.

You have more than one set of attributions and injunctions and you have more than one core belief. If you are having difficulty zeroing in on these, I suggest you copy the lists of attributions/injunctions and the list of core beliefs and put them on your refrigerator. Read them daily and it will come to you.

Once you have identified your core beliefs, it will be important to begin to identify the patterns of behavior you developed that support the core beliefs. In other words, what do you do, or fail to do, that proves these beliefs? If one of your beliefs is "I'm all alone," then do you isolate yourself? Do you find something wrong with everyone so that you can't be close to them? If your belief is "I'm not lovable," do you seek relationships with people who are incapable of loving?

We become experts at proving our beliefs to ourselves because it is critically important to us humans to be able to trust our thinking. So, we develop a complicated set of behaviors that proves our core thinking (beliefs). It will be important to your healing that you do a thorough job of identifying such behaviors.

My Story

The story of my young life can best be described as a mixture of turmoil and scarcity, violence and uncertainty, and an inconsistent mixture of love and happiness. As I describe the impact of my early experiences and the process of the healing that helped me, it is my hope that this will help you understand your own conditioned chemistry.

As a child I lived in a world where my basic needs of food, clothing and shelter were frequently unmet. Starvation, along with physical, verbal and emotional abuse from my father happened on a regular basis, year after year. Some might say that it couldn't have been any worse, but they would be wrong. I was never sexually abused in my home, and I was loved. My experience as a psychotherapist has shown me that there is absolutely nothing worse than growing up believing one is unloved.

Awareness

Leaving home at 13 was a gut-wrenching decision that set me up for anxiety and depression, which I struggled with for years. Although I had escaped the terrible situation of my childhood, I still had the ways of thinking and behaving that came along with me that day I left. The more "normal" my relationships became, the more I realized that I had issues. Because of the inconsistent relationship I had with my father, as well as the starvation and financial deprivation I experienced as a child, my relationships with men, food and money were damaged, distorted and unhealthy, and they began creating difficulty.

After graduating from high school, I went to work, started college at night and began trying to find a partner. I met numerous men that I dated — sometimes for long periods of time — but I was not connecting with them ... my conditioned chemistry just didn't click with theirs. I wasn't aware of my core belief, "I'm all alone" at that time, but it was operating in my relationships with men. I tended to choose men who, like my father, adored me as long as I was pleasing them, and ignored me when I didn't. After several years of experiencing no success in finding someone to marry, I just focused primarily on my work and education. Over time, it became a greater and greater concern that I was not finding a partner.

Additionally, I began to slowly gain weight because I constantly ate large portions that left me feeling stuffed. At home, because food was scarce and we weren't sure when we would eat again, or when food was finally available, we stuffed ourselves and that became a habit. Later, I also became aware that not only had I picked up the overeating habits of my mother, but I was also wasteful like her, with regard to food. I would buy too much produce and end up throwing it away because it spoiled before I could eat all of it. One might expect that with all the poverty in my childhood, we had nothing to waste. But when we had plenty of food, my mother cooked too much and threw away what we couldn't eat.

I found decent-paying jobs, but I could not make my paycheck cover my basic expenses and last until the next payday. I impulsively bought clothing or something I didn't need, then ran out of money for essentials. This was similar to what my dad did when he bought whiskey or something for his car instead of groceries, or coal for our fireplace.

What made me even more miserable was to discover that not only had I developed the impulsive overspending habits of my father, but I was also arrogant like him! When he bought whiskey, it wasn't Heaven Hill, it was Maker's Mark! I constantly left myself broke by insisting on having the best. And, because I had been trained by him to believe that I deserved the best, I surrounded myself with acquaintances and friends who had higher lifestyles than me.

Because we tend to become like those we associate with on a regular basis, I developed a taste for an upper-class lifestyle, which I often couldn't afford. Albeit, I was broke at a higher level than my parents by far, the end result was the same. My awareness of these issues was the first step in becoming healthier. My relationships with men, my overeating and impulsive spending were the first problems I became conscious of as I developed my awareness.

In Summary

Overall, Chapter 5 was designed to give you a starting point, a way to assess a baseline from which to move forward towards the relationships you desire and deserve. It helped you look closely at the heredity, early conditioning and the modeling from your parents and caregivers, which generated core beliefs that were formed in relation to your early circumstances.

In particular, attention was directed to the attributions: what you were told to do or be, and the injunctions: how you interpreted what you should do or be. Attributions and injunctions play a critical role in the formation of core beliefs that entrench themselves into neuron communities, creating the conditioned chemistry from which you operate as an adult.

Understanding your conditioned chemistry is the foundation for change. Negative outcomes are unconditionally tied to negative core beliefs that are operating as your chemistry tattoo. I don't like to tell my clients what they must do, but the fact is, and I am remiss if I don't tell you, you must be willing to assess what is not working in your relationships and become aware of its origins. Only then can you take the next step to work on accepting and letting go of what isn't working.

Chapter Six

Tattoo Removal: Acceptance and Letting Go

"When I let go of what I am, I become what I might be."
— *Lao Tzu*

Once you have a pretty good idea of what your core beliefs are and how they developed, it is time to look at accepting them and letting them go. It's impossible to become someone different without first accepting the reality of who you are now. You don't have to like that reality, but you do have to recognize it in order to change it.

Only when you understand that you developed your negative behavior patterns from your responses to your environment as a child can you say with clarity and acceptance, "Okay, these are the reasons why I'm at this place in my life, and this impasse in my relationships. It's not that I'm not good enough and it isn't because I'm not lovable or valuable. This is the way I am because of what I inherited and learned, and I can let that go and choose something different."

When you realize how and why you have developed as you have, the next step is to become clear about how your conditioned chemistry operates in your relationships. Then you can grieve and release your negative emotions ... the sadness, hurt, anger and fear you feel about your parents or yourself. To begin this process of acceptance and letting go, this chapter will look at working with your inner child, detail several acceptance and letting go exercises, work on parental acceptance and self-acceptance, as well as eliminating the old beliefs.

Acceptance and Letting Go

I want to speak to the idea of an inner child here, as there are those who find it difficult to relate to this term. Neurologically, the way of describing the inner child is that he or she is a neuron community in your brain containing memories, feelings and decisions from childhood. In laymen's terms, your "young self" that is still residing within.

Your inner child can be described in a number of ways. He or she is your fundamental nature, the essence of who you are, your core, your center. This is the part of yourself that knows exactly what you need and don't need, what you like, what you dislike and what you can accomplish. Your inner child is the place from which your creativity and intuition come. A spontaneous, healthy inner child is also where good sex comes from, as good sex is playful and creative. Your inner child is the source of your energy and your spirit. The health and wellbeing of your inner child impacts your relationships in almost every way imaginable.

In Transactional Analysis, there are two primary aspects to the inner child. One is the free child, who is the spontaneous, healthy, creative aspect I just mentioned above. The other is the adaptive child, the aspect of the inner child that is inhibited, serious, stifled. So, with that introduction to the concept of the inner child, let us proceed with the exercises.

EXERCISE I: CONNECTING WITH YOUR INNER CHILD

1. Relax, close your eyes and pick a number between three and ten. Pick the first number that first comes to mind and stick with it. Don't read further until you have picked the number.

2. This number relates to a significant age from your childhood, an age that has a strong connection to your patterns and beliefs.

Look for pictures of yourself at this age and find two significant ones. First, find one where you look happy and spontaneous (free child). Second, choose one where you look constrained, where you have an "I can't be me" or "I can't get what I want" look (adapted child).

3. Remember yourself at this age. Fill in the details. What were you wearing, what did you love to do, who was in your life? Did you have a nickname?

4. Frame these pictures and look at them every day. Note any emotion that comes up. Ask each of these children to speak to you, and then listen internally for what comes. Note any comments like, "You aren't really very smart" or "You don't deserve to get what you want," that come from the adapted child. Lovingly correct this irrational or uninformed thinking with positive statements like, "I really am very smart" and "I do deserve to get what I want."

5. Work with this exercise daily until you feel peaceful and loving towards both children. Until you can hold different, more neutral thoughts about the feelings and circumstances surrounding the adapted child, the "I can't be me" child. Repeat to this child over and over, "You can be you, you are good enough, you are important and you do matter."

Inner Child Acceptance

In the process of accepting who you are and better understanding your conditioned chemistry, it is important to consciously connect with your inner child, the child that formed those beliefs. Getting to know your inner child — both the happy and spontaneous "free child" and the constrained "adapted child" — gives you an opportunity to more fully accept who you are and what you came to believe about relationships as a child. You may find that your free child needs to be re-discovered, or he/

she may just need a little more freedom and attention from you. Your adapted child will need the reworking of his or her negative beliefs in a gentle and loving way.

Look again at your pictures. In the constrained picture, perhaps you were being scolded or couldn't get what you wanted. You might have decided, "I can't be me and I don't matter." This child is the one who adapted to his or her environment as best they could in order to survive, to be accepted and cared for by those in charge of their relationships.

This adaptation is, of course, the root of your negative core beliefs. The child, as it is adapting, is like a miniature adult, trying to figure things out and perhaps feeling lonely, empty, lost or overwhelmed. He or she is the part of you that needs to be nurtured, comforted and healed. It is also the part of you that should not be in charge and at times needs to be lovingly controlled.

In the process of doing this last exercise, it is sometimes helpful to ask your parents about what was going on at home when you were this age. Ask older siblings, aunts or uncles, or anyone who spent time in your home and would know the details about your relationships at that time. The objective here is to uncover the environmental influences that caused you to develop your positive and negative core beliefs.

When you are listening for the voices of each child, pay close attention to what you hear … some of it will be valid information that you need to honor. (Hang in there, I remember how skeptical I was the first time my therapist asked me to do this exercise, but trust me, it works.) Your adapted child might say things like, "You are too critical of me, you take care of everybody else first and leave me out." Work to accept and love this "I can't be me child," and understand that this child is still in the conditioned chemistry of your brain.

Those "I can't be me" neural pathways are deep grooves in your unconscious thinking and responding. Working to accept and redirect the thinking of this inner child is crucial to making change and sets the stage for the serious reworking of your core beliefs that will start in Chapter 7.

Since none of us had a perfect childhood (and if you think you did, dig deeper), you may experience some uncomfortable memories and emotions as you remember yours. These memories are perfectly okay and normal, even desirable. Be gentle with yourself, comfort yourself and get support from those you trust. If you experience feelings that seem overwhelming, please contact a professional for help. It is those unexpressed and unresolved feelings that keep you from moving on to the peaceful relationships you desire and deserve.

Parental Acceptance

Once you have worked on accepting your inner child, it is time to work on accepting the role your parents or caregivers played in developing that inner child. One of the ways I help my clients understand their parents is to utilize a technique called role play, in which I ask them to envision the parent sitting in the room. I coach them in having the conversations they needed, but were unable to have with their parents. Using role play helps clients find their voice ... the one that got buried as they potentially navigated a critical, distant, perfectionistic, weak, violent, depressed, alcoholic, mentally ill or otherwise impaired parent.

This process will illuminate the circumstances and reasons behind the messages you were receiving from your parents. It will give further permission to your inner child to let go of the adapted child thinking. Understanding the specifics of your parental admonitions is a critical part of overall acceptance and change.

EXERCISE II: ROLE PLAY WITH PARENTS

1. First find a couple of objects that you feel are symbolic of your childhood. They could be stuffed animals, pieces of clothing,

pictures, or anything you feel represents a time when you were young and learning about the world.

2. Now cradle that object in your lap, sit in a comfortable chair and relax. Visualize a parent or significant caregiver sitting across from you. Start with whoever comes to mind first, or start with someone who you have very little issue with and start with something easy.

3. Think about what you learned from them, and especially what you learned that was not helpful. Imagine your symbolic objects representing those learned beliefs, such as the stuffed animal you are looking at, a picture or a piece of clothing, and identify what they are saying to you. Perhaps the shirt is saying, "You don't look good in that color" and you have a memory of Mother never being satisfied with the way you looked. Maybe the picture is saying to you, "I'm not good enough."

4. Now look at your symbolic object and say out loud to the parent or caregiver it represents: "That was not true, you were too perfectionistic. I'm not going to listen to you about that anymore." Tell them directly, as though they really are sitting across from you. Tell them exactly how you feel and how the things that they taught you aren't serving you as an adult.

5. Now take your symbolic objects and physically give them back to your parents. Tell them you no longer want or need them, and actually put them back in their laps. Tell them you accept that they did the best they could, that you forgive them, but you are no longer going to operate from those beliefs.

In your mind, it is inevitable that they will try repeatedly to give it back to you. Don't allow it. Make a final decision that you are completely finished with that belief and will not accept it back again. I tell my clients to visualize putting the beliefs away: on the other side of the door with a deadbolt, in a coffin buried under the ground, or wrapped in a tarp and dropped into the ocean ... whatever works.

There are many ways to ritualize the letting go of your negative core beliefs. The previous exercise is one I find extremely helpful with my clients and it consistently nets substantial results. This process can be highly emotional and many people find they need the support of others or a professional to work through their feelings. Don't hesitate to get help if you need it.

The goal of this exercise was to help you further accept your beliefs, yourself and your parents or caregivers. I want you to understand that, as a child, you absolutely did the best you could under the circumstances. In the vast majority of cases, your parents did also. It is only when you reach this conclusion that you are able to forgive and start walking your own life path — that road to freedom ... free of fear of inadequacy, free of the pain of the past and free of failed relationships ... to become your authentic self and live life your own way.

A Word about Self-acceptance

Self-acceptance is one of the most critical elements to creating lasting relationships. I help my clients see that their early decisions about themselves, which made complete sense at that point in their lives, were based on limited cognition and circumstances over which they had no control. The ensuing adaptations to those decisions created behavior patterns that became their life plan and their conditioned chemistry: their chemical tattoos. Some of those decisions and adaptive behaviors work well and some create problems.

All of those decisions have become part of the brain's chemical messengers and are impossible to change without a structured approach. Being unable to bring about change is what brings people to therapy.

Self-acceptance and love are absolutely necessary for sound emotional health, and they do not happen until you can fully accept and forgive your parents and yourself. Acceptance is one of the most critical elements of helping people change and it does not come without understanding. Furthermore, until we fully accept and value ourselves, we may not be capable of making the right choice about a partner.

Old Beliefs

Even after you have come to a place of acceptance and letting go, your old beliefs can lie in waiting, ready for you to fall back into your old ways of thinking. This is easy to do if you aren't diligent in changing those neural pathways. You must reinforce your new beliefs and create an equally strong neuron community that supports these new beliefs.

In every change process there are points where, for a number of reasons, it feels tempting to go back to the old. Everyone can resonate with this temptation. You diet and work hard for a period of time but then seem to fall back into your old patterns. Whether it is because it is familiar, comfortable or just too challenging to sustain the change in beliefs, the old beliefs and patterns can come creeping back unbidden.

Sometimes life will remind us that those old patterns were "true." Your patterns were well established and friends or family members may comment in ways that trigger your old beliefs, causing you to question the validity of this process. That can be an open door for your old way of thinking to come pouring back in.

To help with this, I have my clients design an exercise that works to contain the old beliefs, making it less likely that they will regain a strong foothold in their thinking. This exercise has many varieties that can accomplish the same thing. I will include three different versions, of which you are welcome to pick a favorite and embellish it as you please.

As with any process, one size does not fit all. I find some clients prefer to wade in, accomplishing things in steps or stages, while others like to dive in and get it over in one fell swoop.

The following exercises constitute a range, from wading in with a visualization that can be done in stages or repetitively, to the diving in of the write and burn, where you engage in a single ritual and are done with it. You are welcome to utilize any or all of them in your process of retraining those neural pathways and freeing yourself from your conditioned chemistry.

Given that most people have more than one negative core belief, you may find you want to work on them separately, using different exercises for different beliefs. You may also find you want to work on them all at once, or that one was relatively easy to replace with a new belief, while one in particular is giving you trouble. Experiment with these exercises and find what works for your particular circumstances.

EXERCISE I: CONTAINING OR ELIMINATING YOUR OLD BELIEFS

Option 1. Creative Visualization

Get comfortable, relax and think about the old belief/beliefs that are cropping up. Is there a particular character, someone from a play or someone you make up that represents that old belief? What do they look like? Are they male or female, strong or weak, young or old? How are they dressed, what do they smell like, how are they feeling, what do they sound like? Do they have a name? Visualize this troublesome character in great detail until you can see them clearly in your mind.

Now place them in a setting, as though you are staging a play. Where does this character live? In a cave, on a cloud, in a spaceship, on a mountain? Picture them in this setting.

Next, envision a group of positive characters, helpers if you will, that are additional performers in your image. There could be one or two or a whole group depending on what feels right to you. Again, visualize them in detail. Are they angels or just regular people? Are they representative of the strong parts of you? Are they representative of supports you have in your life? Are they some kind of divine beings? However you envision these helpers is just fine; there is no right or wrong, they just need to be strong enough to help with your troublesome character.

Finally, visualize a way to contain your character with the assistance of your helpers. Perhaps you have visualized your old belief/beliefs as a Dennis the Menace character and your helpers as his parents. Perhaps they can contain him in his room, perhaps even put a lock on the door. In any event, you need to find an image that can contain your character and that feels secure to you. Then, put your character in that contained space and secure him/her in that space.

One client who had core beliefs around "I don't deserve" and "I'm worthless" envisioned her character as a monster of self-hate and self-loathing named Boris. She described him as wearing rags, with long and shaggy hair, dirty with rotten teeth, like a wild man. He exuded self-loathing and, yes, he was a male even though she was not. She saw him as a medieval character living and wreaking havoc in a remote castle. While working with her image she created a moat around the castle so he could not escape, and confined him to a throne in a third floor room. He was strapped in and held down by the queen and two very strong knights.

Over time, as this client worked with her image, she found that her character became less threatening and the restraints could be lifted. Eventually, he became so tame that he was free to walk around the castle. As she integrated her new core beliefs, she was completely able to tame her negative core beliefs.

Use of visualization can be quite powerful in reprogramming your thinking and changing your neural pathways. The image can be used whenever your old beliefs crop up, just go back in and re-contain your character and take away its power to control you.

Option 2. Symbolic Representation

In this version of containing and eliminating your old beliefs, you need to find a picture or object that you feel represents your old core belief/beliefs, and some kind of container to put it in. This process can be done in a formal and ritualized way, or a simple and casual way. You might want to give some thought beforehand to your choice of picture or object. It doesn't have to be a picture of you, but it can be. Or it can be a picture of anything you feel is symbolic of your old beliefs — maybe a picture of you in your old, bad relationship. You might want an object from your childhood or something that you purchased or acquired that is especially representative of you under the influence of your old beliefs.

Once you have selected the item or items, find a time to literally sit down and talk to the object. Tell it that it no longer has any power over you. Say you appreciate that it once played a significant role in your life, but that time has passed and you have moved on. Draw boundaries with your object and hold to them, then put the object in a container (a coffin, if you will) and put it away.

Option 3. Write and Burn

For this particular exercise you will need a piece of paper, a writing instrument and somewhere to burn the paper. This could be a home fire pit, an indoor fireplace or a bonfire. You could even accomplish it with a lighter in an ashtray.

Start by taking your piece of paper and writing your old beliefs out in large, bold script. Add the names — possibly photos — of the relationships you want to remove from your life. Look at each one and feel what the words mean to you. Remember how you felt when they controlled your life. Take a deep breath and prepare to let them go. Sometimes when you let relationships go, they come back to you improved and that's a wonderful experience.

Now burn the piece of paper. Watch the flames dissolve your old beliefs. Watch them turn to ashes. Realize they can never be reconstructed; they are gone. Let yourself believe they are now in the past, and remember this when you are tempted to allow them back.

There are lots of different exercises you can use to continually reinforce letting go of your old beliefs. Some of you may find that focusing on the new core beliefs is enough to remove your old chemistry tattoo. Others will have deeper resistance and bouts of self-sabotage that will require some direct work with eradicating the old beliefs. The point here is for you to know there are numerous tools available that can positively impact your success, so don't give up and fall back into your old beliefs, your old ways of doing things. Utilize the tools in this book.

My Story: Acceptance

When I first entered therapy, I didn't like myself very well because no matter how hard I tried, no matter how many books I read on the subject of relationships, diet or finance, I remained un-partnered and unable to control my eating and spending. I was tired all of the time from over-committing and I constantly isolated myself and felt lonely. I knew I couldn't trust myself with my wellbeing and that was a frightening experience. I was continually cleaning up messes in my life that I had created by choosing the wrong men and overspending, and I was gradually but relentlessly gaining weight.

I started therapy focusing on the trouble I was having in my current relationship. My therapist began the process of helping me discover my core beliefs, accepting and forgiving myself. I learned about the indelible impact of my early childhood experiences. I came to understand that what we experience in our early childhood that is attached to intense emotion and that takes place over a long period of time on a routine basis becomes part of our brain's neural functioning.

So, as a child I was alternately feeling close or alienated from my father, overeating from fear of starvation or watching my father overspend in a desperate attempt to avoid the painful reality of our deprivation. I carried these habits into adulthood as part of my "normal" routine behavior. I had never been able to accept this part of me because I couldn't understand how I had enough fortitude to go out into the world alone at 13 and yet couldn't do something as simple as not eat too much!

The lack of support from my parents and too much responsibility for my age had brought about my decision that, "It's all up to me and I'm all alone," a belief that caused me to take on too much responsibility and to disconnect from close relationships. But my therapist's explanation made sense to me, and I gradually came to accept the reality that my core beliefs were a direct result of my early experience.

Forgiveness

After years of self-loathing regarding my un-partnered status, and my weakness with money and food, I started to form a picture of myself as a child — a little girl doing her best to survive in a terrible situation — and I began to forgive her. My therapist and I did much role-playing with my parents in which I expressed my hurt, sadness and anger at what had happened to me and my siblings as children. I virtually gave their negative influences back to them, and was able to forgive them as I learned to understand them better. Finally, I was able to forgive and truly love myself. It was then that I could truly let go.

Reaching the place of forgiveness and letting go was one of the single greatest experiences of my life, and I want that for you. I have seen this process work for thousands of people and it is still what drives me to go in to my practice every day; I'm still excited about it.

In Summary

This chapter was aimed at helping you understand your core beliefs, what they are, where they came from, how to accept them and how to let them go. I want you to understand that what you have experienced in your relationships, including all your difficulties, makes perfect sense based upon how you developed as a child. Utilizing the exercises included in this chapter can give you a good understanding of your development, and help with the letting go process.

Chapter Seven

Creating Chemistry that Works

*"Never give up, for that is just the place
and time that the tide will turn."*
— *Harriet Beecher Stowe*

Only when you have reached a place of understanding, acceptance and letting go are you free to move on from your old beliefs, your old conditioned chemistry, and replace it with something new and something healthier. With the establishment of positive beliefs, you will make sound choices and beneficial decisions about your relationships. New habits, new behaviors, new goals and new situations need to replace the old ones that were based on your erroneous, conditioned chemistry.

It is now time to get serious about committing to imprinting a new internal chemistry. Ask yourself what you are willing to do, what you are willing to change and what you are willing to give up. If your job or your relationship is based on your old belief system, you may need to change or even replace them.

Ask yourself who you want this new you to be. Think about where you will work and with whom you will associate. How do you want to be treated, how do you want your relationships to feel?

If, in the past, you based your relationships on "not being good enough," people responded accordingly. People may have been critical of you or complained that you didn't do enough. Or maybe they have expected you to do the lion's share of the work in a relationship. These behaviors will no longer fit or feel comfortable. They will no longer be compatible with your new beliefs and will require you to act differently, and, when you act differently, it can rock the boat of established relationships and put into question the role that you previously played.

When you begin the process of integrating these new beliefs, it is important to first create a self-contract from which to operate. These new beliefs and new choices about how you will behave must then be reinforced until they become habitual ways of thinking and acting.

I have included in this chapter a number of ideas to help you structure that reinforcing process. These include: 1) Establishing a new set of core beliefs from which you will operate; 2) Drafting a mission statement/self-contract; and 3) Incorporating the use of affirmations. These relatively simple tools can make a dramatic difference in reprogramming those neuron communities in your brain and are of great importance in your overall success.

I have designated the latter half of this chapter to self-sabotage, those things we all do to shoot ourselves in the foot. Change can naturally stimulate the old patterns and staying conscious of potential potholes is vitally important. Everyone has the capacity to self-sabotage, and frankly, it is an easy trap to fall into if you don't have safeguards against it. This is why we will pay close attention to the various traps people fall into, especially relationship fallout, and incorporate ways to navigate or avoid problems into your awareness.

Establishing this awareness, this new foundation, is essential to creating the change you want, a change that will allow your relationships to be free from those restrictive core beliefs, a life filled with joy and satisfaction. Although there was work involved in discovering and releasing your old core beliefs, this turning point, where you will now fully incorporate your new core beliefs, requires thoughtful concentration. How sturdy your new foundation is will equate to how strong and lasting the new relationships you build will become.

As with any new habit, your new beliefs will require repetition to make them permanent. The information and the exercises in the following sections are designed to support this process and to help ensure your success.

A Decision to Believe Differently

It is time to create a new vision, a new set of positive beliefs to replace your old troublemaking ones, and you do this by making a decision to believe differently. If your entire life has been based on a particular set of beliefs, a new set of beliefs will be required in order to change your life.

To establish this new way of thinking I have my clients make a decision to believe differently. This decision is an essential foundation on which to build your new relationships. This decision starts with a commitment to believe differently about yourself, to choose new core beliefs and consciously incorporate them into your thinking and being. For our purposes, then, the first step is to establish new beliefs in contrast to the old.

EXERCISE I: NEW BELIEFS

Start by writing out a new set of core beliefs that counteract your old ones. Look at your list of core beliefs from Chapter 5 and begin to formulate positive statements in contrast to your negative ones. This is your first attempt at working with your core beliefs. Understand that you may have more clarity as time goes by as to understanding what they truly are.

Start with two or three essential beliefs. For example: If you resonated with the core belief, "I can't be me" or "I'm a burden," you could rephrase these in the positive with statements like, "I can be me" and "I am a blessing." Word them in a way that feels good to you and that works to directly reprogram the previous troublemaking belief. You will have had some experience at this from your inner child exercise in Chapter 6. Do you remember what you countered those negative beliefs with, the ones your inner child said to you? What positive statements naturally came to mind? Write them down and begin to incorporate them into your self-talk.

EXERCISE II: MISSION STATEMENT/SELF-CONTRACT

When you feel satisfied with the new core beliefs that you have chosen, write them into a formal contract to yourself, stating, "I have made a decision that the following statements (write them out) will now constitute my new core beliefs!

You can make this document as fancy or as simple as you please. Some clients like to make an official or visual represent-ation of their new decision and what they will now believe. It is important to ritualize this process and put it down on paper in a way that has meaning for you. You will use this contract as a point of reference while you continue the work of integrating these new beliefs.

This mission statement should declare your new beliefs in a clear, concise and comprehensive manner, such as, "I, Ellen Smith, love me and I accept that I am good enough and it is okay for me to be myself. My relationships are satisfying and long-lasting …"

This mission statement must be taken very seriously with an ironclad commitment to stick to the contract and live by the new beliefs. When my clients respond to this exercise with an, "I'll try" attitude, my comeback is, "Try and pull my finger off." There is no equivocating about this work. There is no trying with this process, just doing. This is an I WILL statement … I will love me and I will accept that I am good enough and I will experience satisfying relationships.

Then complete the contract with what you are WILLING to do in order to realize this commitment. This might include statements like, "I am willing to find a satisfying job" or "I am willing to experience supportive relationships." Add any visual representations that have meaning for you and frame the contract/ mission statement, placing it somewhere you can easily see it and make sure that you read it every day, non-stop for months and years to come.

See below for an example of one client's mission statement.

MY MISSION STATEMENT

I am important and I am lovable. I deserve happiness.
I am at peace. I am joyful and energetic.
I'm calm, healthy and happy.
I will experience mutually loving and supportive relationships.
I will obtain what I need and remove obstacles in my relationships.
I will stay constantly focused on creating my new chemistry tattoo and doing the daily work it takes to achieve it.
My relationships are healthy, satisfying and long-lasting.
Every day, in every way my life, my relationships are getting better and better.

Creating Habitual Thinking

It would be lovely if we could all just decide, "This is my new belief," and relationships would then change accordingly. Unfortunately, those neuron communities are still programmed to play out the old negative core beliefs. So, in order to replace them and build new neuron communities, you must engage in a prolonged process of repetition, a process of reinforcing your new beliefs to create new neural pathways. If you don't do this you will not create lasting change.

It is said that it takes between 21 and 30 days to begin to integrate a new habit, a new way of thinking or behaving. Like me, you are not going to want to hear this, but I must tell you that changing neural pathways takes years. You can get dramatically better by staying diligently focused for 60 to 90 days. However, to create new chemistry that becomes automatic, which is the goal, you should input your new decisions every day for well over a year, and after that review them on a regular basis. I structure this process for my clients with the use of affirmations. These affirmations can be printed and read daily, put on an audio CD and listened to daily, and placed as a message on your screensaver and other locations you see regularly.

EXERCISE I: AFFIRMATIONS

Take a few minutes and write your new beliefs on sticky notes. Remember, changing your beliefs will change your relationships. Let's say, for example, that your negative core beliefs consisted of, "I'm not good enough" and "I can't be me." You will have replaced these beliefs in your new set of core beliefs with something like, "I am good enough" and "I can be myself and I'm okay." Write these affirmations on a number of sticky notes and place them in prominent places in your life. Put them in places you are likely to see them on a regular basis. Put them in your gym bag, on your computer screen and at your office. Put them on your bathroom mirror, on kitchen cabinets, on doors and in your car. Put them on all levels of your home, from the laundry room to the attic.

This may seem silly but you need to convince your brain that this is indeed your new way of thinking, and repetition will help do that. Repetition is the only thing that will change those neural pathways. Your brain is like a computer that can be reprogrammed, and reprogramming is what you must do to solidify your new beliefs.

Reprogramming can be accomplished in many ways in addition to sticky notes: with banners, audio recordings, treasure maps or symbolic objects. You can create a large banner that affirms your new belief/beliefs and place it across your fridge or in the entry of your home. You can record your new affirmations on an endless loop tape or CD and listen to it in the car or as you go to sleep. You can make a collage (treasure map) with sayings and drawings that reinforce these new beliefs. You can ask yourself, "What objects represent this new belief for me" and then surround yourself with those things.

II. Why it's So Important to Reprogram Our Brains

Whether you are operating from your old beliefs or your new ones, they will generate results in your world. Until the new beliefs are established and have overridden the old ones, your results will continue to be predicated on the more dominant, old beliefs. This is why you often hear people commenting that they have recreated a past experience yet again, even when they consciously try not to.

Even when people desire to change, if they don't work to reprogram their brains, they will recreate experiences from the conditioned chemistry of the dominant neuron-driven level. Unfortunately, it is not enough to only hold your new beliefs at a conscious level; you must also change the unconscious level. This is why you hear things like, "I married the same man three times."

We recreate from the same unconscious beliefs, even if we consciously desire something different. Desire alone is not enough to create different results. This is why many of us find ourselves in the same negative patterns over and over again.

How, exactly, does this work? A client of mine, named Nancy, is a prime example. Nancy married the same man three times. Each of them was cold and emotionally indifferent to her. She left each one of them in the hopes of finding something better. But one of Nancy's negative core beliefs was, "I'm not lovable."

She grew up in a family where her parents were not physically affectionate and they did not pay much attention to her. Nancy's conditioned chemistry was to set about proving how her core beliefs were right, in her case marrying men who treated her as if she was unlovable.

Because Nancy's belief system grew into a deeply etched neural pathway, she was unconsciously bound to recreate situations and relationships based on her belief about being unlovable. Without changing the belief and creating new patterns, Nancy had little hope of marrying a man who would treat her differently than her parents did.

This is why it is so crucially important to do the repetitive work of reprogramming your neural pathways. If you want to see real change in your life and relationships, you need to repeatedly reinforce your new beliefs with affirmations and decisions. Creating new beliefs is the way to create a new life, but you must believe those new beliefs and you must establish them as the dominant neural pathways in your brain. Nothing replaces repetition in changing neural programming.

Maintaining the New You

I would love to tell you that repetition alone will create the results you desire, and for some that will be the case. For others, however, they will encounter both resistance and potholes that can stall or even stop the process. For these individuals, more than repetition of the new beliefs will be necessary.

Being armed with a good understanding of these potholes can greatly circumvent backsliding and help ensure success. For that reason this section will examine what you need to know in order to prevent tripping up by taking a look at your new beliefs in the context of your whole life and providing you with tools to ensure success.

Understanding Self-sabotage

Change causes you to become a little disoriented because you are asking your brain to shift gears. Your brain has been on automatic pilot and now you are asking it to shift into something unfamiliar. There is a tightly woven, strongly connected, deeply entrenched neural community that is being interrupted and replaced with this change in core beliefs. Your brain will try to go down those well-worn neural pathways until it has another established option.

Your "old self," your "old brain circuitry," is accustomed to doing things in a certain way and doesn't want to tolerate the discomfort of learning and practicing new behaviors. It will remind you, in the form of excuses and obstacles, why you can't succeed at change. These excuses and obstacles manifest as forms of self-sabotage.

Our brains can become chatterboxes, admonishing us over and over as we try to do things differently. "I've tried dating and never found anyone. I shouldn't bother doing it again." "Nobody really cares anymore what I look like, so losing weight doesn't really matter." "I'm tired and deserve that food." "I've worked hard and deserve that new car" (even though you can't afford it). "I've worked hard enough and need a break from studying" (even though it could make or break your grade).

Like so many parents who become fatigued and give in to the constant barrage of demands from their child, we can be very tempted to give in to the demands of our adapted child, our old neural pathways and capitulate to old behaviors. This is not the right decision, but we must be equipped with foresight and tools to prevent our old way of thinking from inviting our negative core beliefs back.

The Pitfalls of Self-sabotage/Falling into Potholes

In changing your core beliefs, in changing that conditioned chemistry, a whole new world potentially awaits you. With different beliefs you can expect to have very different experiences in your relationships and even to see the world in a whole new light.

This process does not come without its challenges. Many people experience lots of internal resistance to making substantial change and can self-sabotage the process if they are not prepared. Humans are creatures of habit, and as the old saying goes, "Old habits die hard." For this reason, the following sections will include a focus on visualizing the new you in order to combat self-sabotage, an understanding of the fundamentals of self-sabotage, a more in-depth look at relationships, relationship fallout and the need to incarcerate old beliefs. The concepts and exercises in these sections prepare you to move forward with your process in a far more successful manner.

Beginning to Change Your Conditioned Chemistry

How is your life going to be different with your new beliefs in place? How are these new beliefs going to affect your relationships? What kind of support do you need to achieve success and not fall back into old patterns? What will you need to give up?

Self-sabotage potentially occurs when we don't pay close enough attention to these kinds of questions, when we don't have a clear picture forming in our minds. Your beliefs have changed, your relationships will mirror that change and you will need to be flexible. You need to both anticipate and participate in those changes. Let's start by looking at your life with those new beliefs in place.

EXERCISE I: VISUALIZE THE NEW YOU

Close your eyes, take a couple of deep breaths and picture the new you. Do you look different with those new beliefs? Have you cut your hair, changed your clothes or lost weight? Your goal is to be yourself. What does that mean? Do you have a different job, different friends or different habits?

Visualize every aspect of your life. Picture how you look, where you live, who you are close to and what your routines are like. Fill in the details in a concrete image that really feels good to you and work on it daily in conjunction with your affirmations. Building this image will give you a new neural pathway for your brain to draw from. It will further reinforce that new and different set of core beliefs.

The Fundamentals of Self-sabotage

In conjunction with building a strong image of the new you, it is important to strengthen your cognitive understanding of the pitfalls that can occur when trying to make change. Before I suggest ways to counteract these pitfalls in the next chapter, let's consider the primary ways in which we stray from the program into self-sabotage, the things we potentially don't pay enough attention to that can become potholes on our road to success.

1. Not giving yourself enough support. Many people trip themselves up by trying to go through the process alone. It can be a major pitfall to try and carry out this process alone or in isolation.

2. Being Unwilling to give up people or things that don't support your change. Your willingness to move on from unhealthy relationships or let go of things/habits are crucial for successful change. More on this in the Relationship Fallout section.

3. Inability to maintain commitment to your new beliefs. You must stay committed to the process long enough for the new beliefs/decisions/habits to become automatic, habitual. Value yourself enough and decide you deserve to have what you want. Stick with it even if it is taking longer than you want it to.

4. Difficulty staying committed to what's right for you, not what's right for others. Don't let others control you or sabotage you. Examples might include getting ready to exercise and allowing someone else's request for help to cancel your workout. Or working hard to serve a delicious but healthy meal and your partner or family complains so you serve a rich dessert and eat it with them.

5. Challenges staying focused, awake and balanced. You must guard against ignoring your new awareness or putting it on the back burner, allowing yourself to "go unconscious" or become too busy. Examples might include putting too much into your schedule so that the change is too inconvenient; it's just easier to follow the old routines. Another is allowing yourself to become too busy to

stay in touch with what's important to you; i.e., the changes you are trying to make. This is one of the most prevalent reasons people fail to reach their goals. In our frenetically paced society, operating on automatic pilot is part of the cultural mandate aided by numbing factors such as junk food, antidepressants and pervasive two-dimensional technological relating. Monitoring the use of these mind-numbing constructs will aid in your staying focused and your overall success.

6. Lack of understanding or accepting that changes in relationships are part of any change process. The people you love are making LOTS of noise about how they don't like the changes you are making, and you are afraid you'll lose them so you acquiesce, going back to your old beliefs and patterns. Changes in relationships, even relationship fallout, need to be understood and anticipated as part of your change process. Then when others oppose your change you can let them know this is the new you. They can accept it or not, but it may mean the downgrading or even termination of the relationship.

7. Not honoring your contract with yourself. Stay committed to the bigger picture and to building those new neural pathways. If your new belief is "I am worth it," you are generating new behaviors that reinforce that belief. This would likely include better self-care. But when faced with your favorite dessert, you lose touch with your overall contract and eat that piece of cheesecake instead of fruit. This reinforces the old neural pathways rather than building the new ones, which will lead to your overall success.

8. Failure to let go of secondary gain. Whether it's overloading yourself, overeating, overspending, being a doormat or staying confused, there is something about your old behavior that provided comfort, reassurance and secondary gain. For example, eating the cheesecake that is not part of your new plan serves to satiate

loneliness. Thus, it's not the actual eating of the cheesecake, but the secondary gain of emotional comfort that becomes the motivator that sabotages your new behavior.

9. Underestimating the difficulty of change. If you will accept that it took years for you to develop the neural pathways that are causing your trouble, it will be easier to accept that it could take months or maybe a year to develop your new decisions, your new neural pathways. If you think the process will be easier than it turns out to be, you can feel overwhelmed and back off from the challenge. Making the change you truly want and need will require a significant amount of time, energy and possibly emotional upheaval, not only for you but for your loved ones. Allowing yourself to feel overwhelmed is different than being too busy, but they are kissing cousins!!!

10. Doubting that the process works. As you encounter obstacles or difficulties, you may start questioning the validity of the process … whether or not it really works, which can be an open door for resurrecting old beliefs. Hold tight to the awareness that this can work and don't let your doubts derail you.

In combating each of the above-mentioned self-sabotaging possibilities, it is essential to always stop and go back to the original contract you made with yourself; your mission statement for your new life; the "I Will" statement. This overarching or bigger picture concept is what will carry you through all the pitfalls and potholes you encounter in the process.

All of the above factors your ability to succeed at incorporating your new core beliefs and experiencing the life and relationships that come with them. In general, you must pay close attention to all your relationships when in a process of change. This means your relationships with people and with things (habits). How is your relationship with your parents or partners likely to change?

How about your relationship with money, with food or with time? Understanding your changing relationships is important and will be looked at more closely in the next few sections.

Relationship Fallout

One of the first difficulties most people encounter when they are changing is that they experience some kind of relationship fallout. Since this is a book about change that is primarily geared to relationships, I imagine many of you reading this might well need to move on from certain relationships. But, just so you know, some people may move on from you too. This may happen naturally, where old friends or co-workers fall by the wayside, others may require a conscious decision on their part or your part to move on. Essentially, when you start changing, the reactions of the people around you will let you know which relationships are healthy and which ones are just arrangements for someone else's happiness. If you stay grounded in your new beliefs, old relationships will often self-select, meaning naturally fall away.

Being aware, and changing or ending unhealthy relationships can take courage. It is common to feel all kinds of discomfort, agitation and anxiety, which can cause you to give up and return to your old habits. Your relationship with everything is changing, even with yourself. This can unleash a powerful internal resistance and anxiety that often come when we begin making change. Just be aware that this internal resistance is common and you will move through it as you move forward and shift your relationships.

An example from my own life is the relationship I had/have with my old friend, Roberta. Prior to changing my old troublemaking core beliefs, I was a pleaser who operated from, "It's all up to me." I worked to ensure other people's happiness and I always took care of things for everyone around me. So, you can imagine the kinds of people I attracted.

After I worked to change my core beliefs, I began making different and better choices about my life. I quit my job and started a business, and I wasn't helping out with my friends in the same way I had prior. One night I held a small dinner party for friends, including Roberta, in honor of my birthday. In the middle of dinner, Roberta announced, "Mae, you have changed and I don't like it!" I asked, "What do you mean?" She said, "You're different. You're not as giving as you used to be. You've become cold and uncaring."

It was true. I had changed. I used to help her with all kinds of things in her life. I helped her decorate, shop and entertain. I gave her advice and was readily available if she needed me. I always initiated everything and maintained the relationship.

I felt the old fear rushing in. "Oh my God, she's not happy with me. I need to do something!" But then I realized it was my birthday and I didn't want to focus on making her happy! The old me would have tearfully apologized and reassured her how much I loved her, but I had changed. As it was, I had purchased and prepared my birthday dinner and invited her over. She had done nothing for the birthday and now she wanted me to take care of her, meet her needs. Fortunately, I was far enough along in my process that I stood my ground and told her, "I'm doing what I need to do to take care of myself. I'm sorry if that seems cold or uncaring to you."

Later that night, when I had time to reflect on the interaction, I felt sad and shed a few tears, actually a lot of tears. Roberta had meant a great deal to me. But then I got mad and thought, "Relationships are a two-way street and this one isn't!" I realized she wanted me to operate out of my old caretaking patterns, the ones the relationship was founded on, but I couldn't do it any longer. I further realized that our relationship had always been based on what I did for her. Since pulling back to take better care of my own life, she had felt cheated because she wasn't getting as much attention and support from me as she did before. Ultimately, I had to downgrade the relationship.

This story is an example of one of many shifts that took place for me in my relationships after I changed my core beliefs. My life became a lot healthier and not everyone could appreciate or support that. So, like me, you may find that change will have to take place in some of your relationships.

To really examine this in your own life, I suggest the following visualization that I use to help my clients.

EXERCISE I: MAGIC CARPET VISUALIZATION/PEOPLE

Imagine yourself floating on a magic carpet. Everyone in your life is on this carpet. (It's a very large carpet.) Whom do you want to stay? Who would you rather wasn't there? Who feels right in this new life you are creating? Who drains you, who energizes you? Who is supportive of your new way of being?

It may take some time to begin to consciously see what relationships are working and which ones need some altering. As I have said before, some will naturally self-select and fall away; others will require that you discuss the situation and advocate for the changes you are making. As I explained to my friend Roberta, I was changing some unhealthy patterns and my doing less for her was not meant as a slight. It was just about me developing healthier ways of interacting based on a more positive sense of self.

EXERCISE II: MAGIC CARPET VISUALIZATION/CONSTRUCTS

As with your relationships to people, things in your life will naturally need to change. Things, in the form of habits, acquisitions and constructs, will need adjusting as you integrate your new beliefs. If your old life was based on "I'm worthless and don't deserve," for example, the new and "deserving" you may want to take better care of yourself, eat differently, exercise, create more relaxation time. You may not feel comfortable in your old clothes; you may want to change your style of dress, redecorate your house or alter your leisure routines. This may require you to divest yourself of old things and acquire new ones.

Additionally, your relationship to constructs like time and money may need to be adjusted. For example, tightwads who felt they were worthless and didn't spend based on this old belief, may now want to be more generous with themselves based on their new way of thinking. In any event, some things in your life will need to be moved out and others acquired. The previous magic carpet exercise can be used with things as well as people and is a simple way to assess what should be removed from your life and what should be added.

EXERCISE III: MAGIC CARPET VISUALIZATION/THINGS

Again, imagine yourself floating on a magic carpet. Everything in your life is on this carpet. What do you keep? What do you discard? What fits? What doesn't? What do you need in order to make this new life work? Inventory the different areas of your life. Do you need to move? Do you need a different job? Begin to discard the things that no longer work for you and create space for something more appropriate to come in. Take your time and really examine your hobbies, your volunteer commitments, and your home and its contents.

This is an exercise that can be repeated over and over in the months following the shift of your old beliefs. It allows you to assess what you might still be holding onto that has the potential to sabotage your new way of being, the potential to call back your old core beliefs.

In Summary

Overall, this chapter was designed to give you a solid foot-hold from which to integrate your new beliefs, your new life and your new relationships. It looked at consciously choosing your new beliefs and committing to a mission statement, reinforcing these beliefs with affirmations and repetition, creating new habits and understanding the pitfalls of self-sabotage. I included tools to help you structure each part of the process and to work towards changing your neural pathways or conditioned chemistry.

My message here is essentially that the more knowledge you

have about the process, the better prepared you are for the potholes and the more likely you are to step over them and succeed. If I walk down a road and fall in a pothole, I can be derailed, injured and completely stalled in my process of walking down that road. If, however, I am aware and looking for potholes, there is a good chance I will see them and avoid them, greatly increasing my odds of successfully walking down the road.

Being aware of self-sabotage is being aware of potholes. If you stay conscious of the potholes, even anticipate them, you are that much more likely to avoid them. Good luck! In the next chapter we will examine how to pave your road to success, essentially filling in the potholes. This involves building positive supports and underscores success by what I like to call creating "chemistry you can count on!"

Chapter Eight

Chemistry You Can Count On

"Motivation is what gets you started.
Habit is what keeps you going."
— *Jim Rohn*

How do you create permanent, positive change in your relationships? How do you create chemistry that you can count on? How do you guarantee the results you set out to obtain? Change is a process that requires developing new habitual routines and new habitual thought patterns to replace the old ones that have limited your relationships. It is your habitual routines and habitual thoughts that etch neural pathways into your brain and create conditioned chemistry. The purpose of this book is to help you create a chemistry tattoo that you can count on to give you positive results.

In the previous chapter, I alluded to the difficulty of this process — of any change process — and the importance of structuring your life to support permanent change and a permanent alteration of your brain chemistry. If you truly decide to succeed on a diet, you don't fill the house with sweets and chips, you don't hang out with friends who encourage you to overeat and you don't go to a buffet every night for dinner. These things would reinforce your old conditioned chemistry. I don't like to tell my clients what they must do; however, this is a situation where I would be seriously negligent if I didn't. So, here it is …

If you want to succeed at creating change in your neurochemical programming, you must institute structures that reinforce your new beliefs and behaviors.

So far, this book has placed emphasis on understanding concepts, and on working to change beliefs and brain chemistry. In the process of understanding those concepts you have made a decision to embrace new and more supportive beliefs, and to change your conditioned chemistry for more positive results. You have an understanding of the pitfalls and resistance, the self-sabotage and relationship fallout that all routinely come with making significant change. Now it is time to examine strategies that will dramatically increase your chances of long-term success, strategies that will permanently alter your brain chemistry.

In this chapter, we will look at life and relationships free from your old conditioned chemistry. What does that look like for you? How will you ensure that you can get there? How will you gauge success? The first section of this chapter will detail ten strategies that counteract the self-sabotage mechanisms mentioned in Chapter 6. These strategies will be examined in detail and described with short, real-life examples to help you create a portfolio of approaches for changing your conditioned chemistry. In brief, these ten strategies include: 1) Developing and using your support system; 2) Staying focused on basics; 3) Creating an "awake" lifestyle; 4) Self-check-in; 5) Managing your triggers; 6) Managing your relationships; 7) Personalizing the process; 8) Working with your senses; 9) Drawing on your spiritual beliefs; and 10) Self-care. All of these constructs can be integrated over time, and not only will they support change, but they will enhance your relationships in ways you never imagined.

The latter part of this chapter will examine your goals for change and give you a chance to assess your progress. Without some way to measure forward movement, it can be difficult to stay motivated and persist throughout the process. Progress, in and of itself, is a great motivator. Especially when the road becomes difficult, we all need the ability to evaluate our success and to gauge our growth. The concluding portion of this chapter is dedicated to just that and will give you clarity about your progress.

Strategies for Success

The following suggestions are not the "be all/end all" of success strategies that one can employ to help change conditioned chemistry, but they are the top ten that I see work with my clients. Change is a complicated process and we all wish for a simple, magic pill formula to create what we desire. Unfortunately, it doesn't work that way. If it did, the formula would have been bottled and sold long ago. We see evidence of how complicated change is with the myriad of self-help books on the market today, and the plethora of available options to create desired change. So many options exist because so many fail. I was motivated to write this book because I see consistent results with my clients and I know this process works. If you have made the effort to understand and replace your negative core beliefs, you are ready to utilize these strategies for success. If you employ a majority of them on a consistent basis, your success is guaranteed.

1. Developing and Using Your Support Systems

Human beings were meant to be interdependent; it is how we learn, live and love. We exist in relation to others, and others play a significant role in our success or failure. We all have people in our lives in the form of friends, family members, partners, co-workers and neighbors that form formal and informal support systems around us. It is important to take a look at how these support systems are working in your relationships, and make some conscious decisions about how you utilize the people around you.

What is a support system? For the purposes of this work, we are defining it in the general sense of the people around you on a regular basis. A support system consists of a series of situations with others that creates a structure: a once-a-week therapist session, a once-a-month clergy visit, Thursday morning coffees with acquaintances, a daily call to a close friend. Who you surround yourself with will make a huge difference in your ability to succeed and successfully change your chemistry long-term. When you want to make change, you need to surround yourself with people who are where you want to be and people who will support a healthier you.

Although I have stated that some people will naturally fall away when you create change, it is essential to consciously inventory both the friends and family in your life. You need to see how people respond to your new belief system and your different results. Do they embrace the new you, are they skeptical, critical or, worse, undermining? I teach my clients to be aware of how the people around them either support or sabotage their new chemistry. If certain individuals can't support your change and don't naturally fall away, move them to a more appropriate place in your relationships. For example, some close friends may need to become more distant acquaintances. They might become friends you only see once or twice a year. The following are things to keep in mind when assessing your support system.

1. Who are your people? By this, I mean the people in your life who support you, uplift you, with whom you can truly be yourself even in the process of change. It is important to be thinking about this in relation to everyone — from personal relationships, to work colleagues, to your cleaning lady, from your dentist to your mechanic.

2. Choose someone — a professional or trusted friend — to hold you accountable. Share your contract for change with them and formalize their commitment for support … shake hands, sign a contract, ritualize it in some way.

3. Have a short mental or written list of at least two people who will genuinely encourage you, so you have someone to contact when you need support.

4. Make sure that the people you reach out to are trustworthy. Really check that they have your best interest at heart, not their own.

5. Enlist the help of people who will challenge you to stay focused.

6. Do not confide in or depend on people who are needy, critical, jealous, wishy-washy or self-absorbed.

7. Establish regular visits with supportive family or friends to discuss your progress.

For example, my client, Robin — a young mother with three children — created a support structure for her change process that looked like this. She called her best friend, Mindy, daily, took a weekly walk with a minister friend and attended a Wednesday night women's group in which everyone worked on their contract for change. This structure helped her stay connected to her process and reinforce, through the support of others, the work she was doing.

One additional thing I ask my clients is, "Do you know someone who has successfully done what you are trying to do, and can you build a relationship with that person?" Robin originally had core beliefs that included, "I'm not good enough" and some of her resulting beliefs and behavior patterns included not taking very good care of herself. In her process of change, she had committed to better self-care with diet and exercise. As part of her support system, it was very helpful for Robin to have people around her who had successfully integrated a healthy diet and exercise into their lives — people who could both model and directly support her new chemistry. The process of getting support in the form of positive reinforcement and modeling from others cannot be overestimated. This process is an essential part of creating your new chemistry tattoo.

II. Staying Focused on the Basics

Go back to the basics of your self-contract whenever you have a setback or experience resistance or doubt. Resistance, doubt or fear can manifest either internally or externally. When internal, you can experience feelings of resistance or a lack of motivation. When that happens, consider your negative core beliefs and see if they are involved with your resistance.

When the resistance manifests externally, it can come from the people and circumstances around you that threaten to undermine your progress. For example, if your spouse continually complains that you are no longer taking care of things the way you used to, don't revert to your old patterns because there is resistance to change in your relationship. Explain to your spouse that your new decision (i.e., to take better care of yourself) doesn't allow time for all the things you once did, and suggest that he or she find a way to take care of those things. Revisit your contract and let your decision change your circumstances; do not let your circumstances undermine your decision. The very core of this process lies with your decision to live by your new set of core beliefs. At some point you will question your progress, and when that happens always go back to your basic contract and goals.

An example of going back to basics can be seen with my client, Walter. Walter is a 33-year-old single man who has continually failed in relationships with women largely due to his tendency to find fault, criticize and withhold commitment. He made a decision to give up perfectionism and his relationships improved. Sometimes he fell back into old routines and had to go back to the basics of his decision to be more accepting and forgiving of himself and others. When he revisited the basics and worked consciously at affirming his new beliefs, his relationships always improved.

Change is a process, not an event. In my practice, I've experienced many clients who came in and excitedly announced, "I've had a breakthrough," "I'm a changed man" or "I'm a changed woman." And while I'm excited with them and for them, what I know is that it is not the dramatic moments that create lasting change. It is the consistent repeating of affirmations and new behavior patterns over an extended period of time that creates lasting change by reprogramming the very chemistry of your brain.

You may need to do your affirmations again and again, or perhaps you have not been practicing them at all and it is time for another round. Change is like peeling an onion. You may want to start by peeling one layer and then coast for a while, integrating the changes from that layer. Then you may feel the need, the call, to peel the next layer. It is not a different belief that needs to be tackled, but a deeper layer of the same belief. Go back to your basic contract and do your affirmations. This is the bedrock of your success strategies.

III. Creating an "Awake" Lifestyle, Conquering the "Treadmill"

Many of us can't stay focused on what we really want, and can't readily create the change we desire because we are too busy. Our lives are like a treadmill. We are constantly trying to keep up with all the distractions of modern life. For real success with this process, we must become keenly aware of the parts of our lifestyle that interfere with time for contemplation and change.

In my practice, I see couples trying to keep their marriages together, singles searching for love and connection, and children afraid their families will dissolve. They all wonder how things will turn out and how to make their lives work. Like many of us, they are trapped in today's chaotic maze of activities: schoolwork, careers, mortgages, car payments, blended families and the insidious invasion of technology that all work to keep us on a treadmill.

Modern human beings have become isolated from each other with little time to devote to satisfying, successful relationships. Virtually all of the people I see in my practice are struggling with some form of relationship dissatisfaction. "Our greatest joy, and our greatest pain, comes in our relationships with others." — Stephen R. Covey

A primary contributing factor to our inability to create change and experience the positive relationships we all desire is this "too busy" life that most of us are living. Creating change requires time ... time to stop and think, to contemplate and evaluate, time that most of us simply don't have. We exist in a frenetically-paced culture driven by materialism, which devours the days of our lives, leaving no time for face-to-face connections with others. We get up in the morning and hit the ground running. We drive carpools, work at our professions, go to church, run errands, make meals, volunteer, clean house, grocery shop and pay bills. We manage our homes, our jobs, our families and our recreational lives. We deal with financial challenges, political unrest, war and health concerns. We work to look good, stay in shape, eat right, live right and do right. The media is constantly telling us what we should have, wear, do, be and think, and we chase these things in a frenzied fashion, leaving us little time to stay focused on what really matters, especially when creating change.

To overcome this treadmill life, we must all work to stay awake to our commitments, and assess the quality of what we feed ourselves in terms of actual food and information. You can start by looking at your schedule and trying to downgrade all your commitments. Begin by memorizing the following statements for use in keeping yourself less busy:

"I would love to say yes, but I have to think about it."
Or
"I'll need to see if I can work that into my schedule."
Or
"I'll need to sleep on it and let you know."

This gives you time to consider, "Do I really want to do it? How does it fit with my new decision? Does taking on this commitment honor my new contract? Will I be too busy to be truly focused on what I really want?" When you need to say no, start with a positive and say, "I'd love to do that for you, but I just can't work it into my current schedule."

In addition to keeping yourself awake to the level of your commitments, it is important to assess your general quality of life. Are you eating good food versus junk food? Are you exercising, drinking enough water, getting enough sleep, reading rather than sitting in front of the television, spending time in nature, getting fresh air? Chemicals in your food, lack of fresh air and sun, junk food, for the mind, like TV, all help create a veil over the consciousness and inhibit successful change. When you are chronically fatigued from the chemicals you ingest, and the resulting lack of nutrition, your brain doesn't have the energy to form new neural pathways, and it just defaults to the old ones containing the old habits. All of these things affect your ability to stay aware of what is happening around you, how people are treating you and the progress you are making.

Our modern lifestyle can make it difficult to give ourselves the nourishment we need. My client, Carl, is a perfect example. Carl lives alone in the suburbs in a townhome — a twin home, exactly like all the others in his development. He rises in the morning, microwaves an instant breakfast, gets into his car and navigates rush-hour traffic. He parks in an underground parking lot, takes the elevator to the 14th floor, and works all day in front of a computer screen. He eats lunch from a vending machine and stays in his building all day. He ends work and once again navigates rush-hour traffic. He gets fast food for dinner, which he eats at home in front of the television. He goes to bed exhausted, only to do it all over again the following day.

Carl's example might be extreme, but most everyone can relate to elements of it. Where are you compromising the quality of your health and wellbeing? I can't emphasize enough the need for a healthy, nurturing, supportive lifestyle, especially when we are attempting to change brain chemistry. Support your new chemistry by controlling your schedule and commitments, and increasing the quality of the food and information you take in.

IV. Self Check-In

Studies indicate the single most important success factor in the change process is consciously checking in with yourself every day to see how you are doing in relation to your contract. As you are able to better control your schedule and keep your life less busy, it should be relatively simple to find a time to check in with yourself every day. I know that many of you are thinking, "You don't understand, I'm way too busy!" But, remember, I have given you tools to unclutter your busy life, so checking in with yourself can be part of your morning and evening routine, or done while driving, using the restroom or cooking dinner. Make it a habit to start and end your day by taking ten to 15 seconds, breathing deeply and asking yourself, "How am I doing?" Pay close attention to the answer, really listen to yourself and make adjustments as necessary.

I asked a friend who was a nurse from a diet clinic, "What do you see work most effectively with your clients?" She confirmed that those individuals that made the time to weigh themselves and chart their food, checking in daily to assess progress and pitfalls, were unequivocally the most successful at losing weight and keeping it off permanently. The daily check-in works to change conditioned chemistry, which reinforces the new brain patterns and ensures long-term success.

An example of this is happening with my client, Joanie. She developed a system of checking in with herself by setting an alarm on her smart phone that went off twice a day, reminding her to breathe deeply. She had a core belief, saying, "I am all alone," which had created an anxiety condition in her neural chemistry and caused her to breathe shallowly throughout her life. Her new decision was, "I have lots of support." And, twice a day, she reminded herself of this new reality by relaxing, breathing deeply and saying her affirmations, which added building blocks to her new neuron community.

V. Managing Your Triggers

Become an expert at knowing and managing what triggers you, essentially being aware of what can trip you up. Again, if you are following a new food plan and are working to avoid things that might potentially pull you off your designated course, you might avoid going to certain venues to eat, avoid certain challenging social situations that entice you to overindulge and plan not to let yourself get too hungry. There are all kinds of triggers — emotionally and physically — in our lives, triggers that can threaten to pull you back into your old beliefs. These triggers might be interacting with people who treat you a certain way, rejection, being over-controlled, seeing a certain movie, or a given situation. You need to take the time to assess what triggers you.

For a real-life example, one of my clients, Ellen, was dealing with deprivation: fear of never having enough. She had worked hard to create a new belief that she had plenty and to break her pattern of being triggered by the deprivation and overspending. However, when she wasn't careful about monitoring and releasing deeper layers of deprivation as they came up, she was easily triggered into once again overspending. This could result in additional triggers when, for example, a low checking balance or an inadvertent overdraft could bring back her old thinking that there will never be enough, thus sabotaging her new decision. Ellen needed to be aware and stay on top of her triggers, so as not to not engage in behavior that threatened her progress.

We cannot change what we cannot understand. It is vitally important to be aware and monitor your triggers ... to be able to say I know that if I go into that store, the temptation to spend will be too great. I know that if I eat at that buffet, it will be too difficult not to overeat. I know that if I meet my girlfriends at that bar, I will be tempted to drink too much. Protect yourself. Parents do it for their children; it becomes our job to do it for ourselves as adults.

One of my clients, Libby, described how spending time in her family home with her abusive mother was a powerful trigger to overeat, especially the bowls of candy present throughout the house. I advised her to alert herself to that fact and be aware of it before accepting invitations to her mother's home. We decided that she would move the bowls of candy to another room, out of her sight, before beginning her visit. Just being aware of this trigger empowered Libby to make changes that eventually created a new chemical tattoo, allowing her to be around her mother without overeating. Start paying attention to your triggers in relation to the new beliefs you are integrating.

VI. Prepare Yourself for Relationship Fallout!

Remind yourself that relationship fallout may be the price for your new and healthier way of being. It may also be the prize, as it opens you up to have much more positive relationships.

Not to belabor the diet analogy (Can you tell I've had to lose weight in my life?), but when you make a change to healthier eating habits, you may want to stop buying certain foods or you may want to find healthier versions of old favorites. This is also the case with relationships. Just as certain foods may not support your beliefs about yourself as fit and healthy and need to be discarded, certain people will not support your new and healthier beliefs about yourself and may need to be discarded as well. This is a natural part of change and should be anticipated, even prepared for. You might want to survey the people in your relationships and ask, as you did with your busyness and commitments, "How do these people support my new decision?"

My client, John, provides a perfect example. John had a core belief of, "I can't be me." He had been raised in a very strict atmosphere, was the firstborn and expected to follow in his successful father's footsteps in the corporate world. Precipitated by a midlife crisis and divorce in his 40s, he decided to become who he really was. He found that he was creative, interested in psychology and was not really driven to make money or be a part of the corporate world. The problem was, he had developed a circle of friends and family much like his father, who reinforced the corporate lifestyle. So when he decided to change, he experienced a lot of relationship fallout.

Staying conscious about relationship fallout is extremely helpful to the emotional and psychological change process, and it helps support the necessity to move on from certain relationships. You are not as inclined to hang onto a relationship that doesn't support you, and you are not blindsided when people leave if you understand that changing relationships is a natural part of any change process. As well, being aware of relationship fallout can empower you to end unhealthy relationships.

VII. Personalizing the Process

Find new and different ways to make it happen. This is an invitation for you to get creative and use your own life, talents and interests. Use your existing gifts to create representations of the new you. As I mentioned before, the list in this chapter is not exhaustive, and I am always amazed at the creative and interesting ways my clients invent to reinforce and maintain their new beliefs. Personalizing the process in a way that reinforces your new beliefs can look like creating music, poetry or prose, or redecorating your house, changing the way you dress, the car you drive, the place you live, the routines you follow. One client, Jenny, wrote poetry exemplifying the change from her old self, who believed she wasn't good enough to her new self, who believed she was good enough, important and unique.

VIII. Unconscious Imprinting with Visual and Auditory Supports

Beyond the strictly cognitive learning, we need to use supplemental processes to reinforce the new chemistry. Visual and auditory supports can help imprint the new decisions into our brain, creating those new neural pathways and that generate desired outcomes.

This can be done in a variety of ways. One client, Cori, had me make a CD containing her decisions and affirmations. She listened to it each morning upon awakening and each evening before going to sleep. My previously mentioned client, John, put sticky notes all over his home, car and garage. The notes contained his new decision in the form of written affirmations. For example, the new decision for John was, "I am me, and I am important." Some of his affirmations were, "I'm not responsible for others," "I am free to be me," and "I deserve freedom and happiness." He put these messages on sticky notes on his bathroom mirror, on the sun visor in his car, on his laptop as a screensaver, on his refrigerator — places he could think of that he was certain to see every day.

One technique that clients have found very effective is to create a collage or treasure map with visual representations of who they are, what they look like and what surrounds them in their new life. For example, if John were to make a treasure map of his life after corporate America, it might include creative symbols like him engaged in painting, drawing or writing and surrounded by relationships and the things he loves that reinforce who he wants to be. This collage or treasure map could include images of John in various activities, with new possessions, people and accomplishments, and is something to be placed in a prominent position in his home so he can look at it throughout the day, every day! Use magazines, catalogs, posters and photos to create a mural of how you want your life and relationships to look.

IX. Drawing on Your Spiritual Beliefs

Most of us have had occasions where we have felt connected to something beyond our everyday physical reality, a form of divine presence perhaps or a force larger than ourselves. Whether you have an active spiritual practice or not, it helps to believe that something greater than you can help carry this process.

There are basic spiritual practices that transcend any given religion, and can be very supportive when changing brain chemistry. This topic could be an entire book, but suffice to say that at the top of the list is prayer and meditation. Prayer being the active talking to and thanking a higher presence for the good in your relationships (the changes you are making), and meditation, the active listening process that can connect you to divine wisdom and inspiration.

In my experience, my clients who are willing to express gratitude daily and stay connected to some form of higher power find it easier to move their lives in the direction they want to go.

X. Self-care

Reinforcing new and healthier ways of being in the world requires self-care. You can't adopt new and more positive ways of thinking about yourself without paying attention to the way you take care of yourself: physically, mentally, emotionally and spiritually. People that believe they are worth it take time to treat themselves accordingly. They pay attention to their appearance and hygiene; they eat right, exercise, take time to rest, to meditate, to get massages. They surround themselves with positive input, involve themselves in the world, read for enjoyment and develop interests.

My client, Sharon, found that as she began reinforcing her new core belief of, "I'm lovable, valuable and important," her self-care began to change. Always rushing and trying to please others, she began to take time for herself: long walks, relaxing baths, trips to the spa. And the more she reinforced her new beliefs with self-care, the more she reinforced her new chemistry tattoo. Treating herself well encouraged others to do the same and she saw a marked improvement in her relationships as well.

In summarizing this section on success strategies, let me just state once again that these are not the "be all/end all" of things you can do. However, it is easy to see that if you employed even a few of these strategies, your relationships could not help but change for the better. I encourage my clients to pick a couple to start with and work with those until they become routine, then add more. This process is all about feeling better and creating successful, lasting relationships based on engaging in what you really love, being who you really are and having others relate to that person.

Assessing Progress/Gaging Growth

If you want things in your relationships to change, you have to change things in your relationships. That is a given, right? But how do you know that the change is really working? How do you assess your results? And why is it important to do so? Let's take a look at some basics of assessing your progress.

Is change really happening?

You are engaged in this process of changing your conditioned brain chemistry because you did not like the way you felt, the results you were getting, the relationships you were having. The goal, then, is to feel differently, experience different results and have more satisfying relationships. In order to know if you are achieving these goals (and thus successfully reprogramming your neural pathways), you must pay attention to how you feel, look at your results and honestly look at your relationships.

Some aspects of assessing change are very tangible, very concrete and, thus, easy to measure, while others are considerably more subtle. It is crucial for the psychological process of changing your conditioned chemistry that you know the change is occurring. In order to concretely know this, you must pay attention to the process, have specific goals that indicate you are progressing, and be attuned to intricacies and details.

If, for example, you want to lose weight and look better, you can get on the scale every morning and have a tangible assessment of whether or not you are losing the weight. If you are dropping pounds, then, yes, you are progressing with your goal. But you may also be receiving more subtle feedback from the world around you that you are reaching your goal. Your clothes may fit looser, you may have more energy or people may be commenting on how great you look. Pay attention to the evidence you have that your change is occurring.

If your goal is to have a loving, committed relationship when you have been single and alone, an overt assessment could be the engagement ring on your finger. But you could still be having success with changing old patterns if you are feeling attracted to other people, meeting eligible singles, engaging in flirtations or feeling compelled to join a dating service. We tend to frame our goals at the end point, at the result. I will weigh 120 pounds or I will find a partner, but much of how we know the change is working has to do with more incremental steps in the goal achievement process. In answer to the question, "Is change really happening?" You know the change is real if things are changing in a positive direction towards your goals.

How do you assess your results?

Because it is easy to focus on what we are not getting and easy to fall back into the conditioned chemistry, it helps to set a series of reachable goals that you can monitor. My overall goal may be to lose 40 pounds and fit into a size 6, but if I make a series of goals — first to lose 10 pounds and get down one size, etc. — then I can assess my results in a continual and reasonable fashion.

Sometimes our minds project unrealistic goals that we never fully reach, and if, every day, all I can think about is that I haven't lost the 40 pounds, or when am I going to lose the 40 pounds, the process can be undermined. Maybe in the long run I will only lose 35 pounds, but likely I won't even get there if I don't celebrate my success along the way. Losing half a pound is a success, not an "I only lost half a pound."

To further the example of wanting a relationship, you might make your new decision, practice all your affirmations, set up support strategies, and at the end of a year be without a partner. But maybe you have dated three different people, been asked out numerous times and gotten lots of good feedback from others about your changing relationship skills. You may notice that, although you haven't found "the one," you are experiencing a far different quality of connection with the people you have been dating. Progress is not just an end result, it is a process of positive change.

In further assessing your results, it greatly helps to document some of the process. Keep notes or a journal in relation to what is happening. Chart your weight and size changes along with all the comments you get from people around you if you are trying to lose weight and get healthier. Make notes on a calendar about all the dating you have done and how it is going. Describe in writing how you are feeling and how successful you have been in reaching all the stages in route to your goals. Plan little celebrations and reward yourself for your progress, like a pedicure or a new outfit for losing 10 pounds, or an afternoon off to do whatever you like for having gone out on a third date, etc … be good to yourself in this process!

Why is it important to track your results?

Tracking your results works. Tracking your results creates a different level of consciousness that greatly improves your outcomes. It keeps you awake and engaged in the process, prevents backsliding and lets you recover quickly if you do backslide. It reinforces your motivation, provides concrete evidence as to why you are going through the process and whether it is working, and greatly increases the likelihood that you will permanently reprogram your brain chemistry.

When I enter into a contract for change with a client, I ask them how they will know when they are finished. What evidence will they have that their work is completed? This concrete assessment of what change looks like for them is crucial, especially to prevent regressing into old chemical pathways. Until you have actually lived several months, even a year or two, operating from your new decisions, old habits can creep back and sabotage your progress.

For example, my client, Brent, a 42-year-old divorcee, had to tackle a potential sabotage. Overall, his relationships were going well. He had worked out parenting time and a property settlement with his ex-wife. He had identified and accepted his participation in the problems that caused the failure of his marriage, namely, that he was a workaholic and rarely available to his family. Brent established goals to develop his personal life and find a balance between work and leisure. He was making great headway and tracking his progress. He had developed a social life away from work and was focusing on balance. In addition, his career was on the upswing.

One day he announced in his session that he had just accepted a promotion. He felt he had met his goals and was ready to graduate from therapy. However, I was concerned and the contract I make with my clients is that they will stay with the process until we both agree they have completed the work.

I asked Brent to tell me about his promotion and how it fit with his new decision to create a healthier balance between his personal relationships and his career. The look on his face told the tale! His promotion could sabotage his new decision, as it would have him travelling even more and supervising more people. Having recently started a new relationship with a woman who had become important to him, Brent reconsidered the promotion and turned it down, instead staying committed to the balance he knew would create healthier relationships.

In Summary

This chapter was intended to help you look at strategies that reinforce your new beliefs, strategies that create chemistry you can count on, a new chemistry tattoo that will generate your desired results. You begin by developing and committing to a vision of what your relationships would look like with this new chemistry. Now you need to take that vision and develop some structures to reinforce it.

I have suggested a number of ways to reinforce your new beliefs and get better results with your desired outcomes. These ideas included assessing your support systems; taking the time to refer back to the basics of your contract and new decision; working to stay awake by monitoring your time and intake of food and information; regularly checking in with yourself about how you are doing; anticipating what kinds of things will trigger you; assessing your relationships and the role people play in your getting healthier; making this process personal and meaningful to you; working with your spiritual beliefs for support; and focusing on good self-care.

You don't need to do all of the aforementioned, but really commit to two or three that appeal to you and turn them into habits that are as automatic as brushing your teeth. The use of support strategies combined with a conscious effort to track your progress and monitor your results will ensure success. Continually developing these strategies will ensure creating chemistry you can count on.

CHAPTER 9

A New Chemistry Tattoo: Happy Endings

"Though no one can go back and make a brand-new start,
anyone can start from now and make a brand-new ending."
— Carl Bard

In this chapter, I give you examples from the lives of a few of the courageous people who honored me by allowing me to help them make choices about their personal journey. Their names and circumstances, of course, have been changed. People who come to therapy are not the only people with problems. Quite the contrary, all people have problems. Everyone could benefit from the support and advice of a skilled, objective professional. The people who choose to participate in therapy are exceptional; they are not willing to live a "settled for" life. They have moral fiber, spirit and courage. Over the years, I suspect I have learned much more from them than they have from me, but either way, their commitment to personal growth allowed me to pay it forward to those who came after. That is the incredibly significant gift of all those who have sought therapy: they have helped to build the foundation for our understanding of the human psyche and we owe them an incalculable debt.

Case Studies

SOPHIA

Core Beliefs: "I'm all alone and I'm not good enough, no matter how much I do or achieve."

Sophia came to see me as a result of a phone call from her mother, saying, "My daughter is having panic attacks and needs your help." A young actor, Sophia was living her dream studying acting in Los Angeles. She lived in an apartment and took a bus to school. Intelligent and disciplined, Sophia was always on a diet, struggling to maintain a weight that her acting coach would find acceptable. She had also become sexually active with her boyfriend and was terrified for her parents to find out.

Family History

Born and raised in the Southwest, Sophia was from an upper middle-class family. The youngest of two girls, there was a five-year difference between Sophia and her older sister. Because she was so much younger than her sister, she wasn't allowed to participate in most of her sister's activities. Sophia began feeling left out and lonely. She began developing conditioned chemistry that said, "I'm all alone."

Sophia's father was a successful, hard-working attorney who had always wanted a son and expected a high level of performance out of his daughters. Her mother, a perfectionist, was overly critical of her daughter's looks and performance. Sophia had been an honors student her entire life, but she told me she had been criticized and second-guessed by her mother for "as long as I can remember." This had created conditioned chemistry and the beginning of another core belief in Sophia that sounded like, "I'm not enough, no matter how much I do or achieve."

Sophia attended a high school specializing in acting, where she did very well. She had met and acted with a young man who absolutely adored her and couldn't seem to get enough of her, which was powerful foodstuff for her core belief, "I'm all alone." Although Sophia was usually the first actor to learn and execute her role, her acting coach was never satisfied with Sophia's weight, and almost never chose her for the leading role. Sophia dutifully and diligently, even obsessively, tried one food plan after another.

Sadly for her, her acting instructor just kept giving Sophia the message, "You're too fat, and not good enough."

Sophia began to realize that no matter how hard she worked, no matter how much weight she lost, she would never be good enough for her acting coach. She needed to begin thinking about a career change, but she was worried about what her parents would think and, thus, found it difficult to make a decision. Her early conditioned chemistry said, "I'm all alone. No matter how much I do, it won't be enough and I'm not good enough." Now in her adult life, she had chosen circumstances that reinforced this. She had an acting coach who gave her a repeated message of "You're not good enough," her family continued to espouse high achievement values with no "permission" in life to quit, and she was partnered with a person who her family liked but didn't see as an appropriate partner. Sophia was, quite literally, stuck.

Presenting Symptoms

Sophia began by talking about her panic attacks. Many of them happened on the bus on her way to rehearsal, others happened when she was alone. She described a racing heartbeat, sweaty palms and tightness in her chest. She had trouble breathing and was afraid that she might pass out or be unable to get home, or worse, she might even die. She had originally called her mother in tears, not understanding what was happening to her. "What can possibly be the problem?" she asked me. She had always wanted to be an actor, and now she was in acting school. She couldn't understand why she was experiencing so much anxiety and panic.

Therapy Process

I spent the first few visits defining the problem and clarifying Sophia's early history. Both parents had anxiety-related conditions that could have easily genetically predisposed Sophia to her panic attacks. Next, I asked her to say more about her anxiety and panic attacks. For example, how long had she been having these symptoms? Did she remember feeling this way as a child? I asked her to close her eyes and see if she could picture a situation in her early life when she was feeling anxious. I asked her to pay attention to what she was thinking and what she was saying to herself when she was feeling anxious. Then I asked, "What do you need to obtain and what do you need to give up, in order to free yourself of this anxiety? How do you want to be different and what stops you from getting what you want?"

We found that some of Sophia's very earliest memories of feeling anxious related to being excluded from the activities of her older sister. When she asked repeatedly to go along, she received the unchanging explanation from her mother, "You can't because you are not big enough, or you're not old enough, or you don't understand enough." At age two, Sophia's neural development didn't offer her the ability to understand that there was nothing wrong with her. She couldn't figure out that the problem simply lay in the significant age difference between her and her sister. So, because of Sophia's limited ability to comprehend the situation, the frequent and recurring messages started to formulate a belief within her brain that said simply, "I'm not enough and I'm all alone," which evolved into "I'm not good enough and I'm all alone." Because Sophia's parents loved her and showered her with attention individually, she did not develop the belief that she was unwanted, as she might have.

Sophia's situation with her acting coach had engaged and activated her early decision about not feeling good enough. Her relationship with her partner had removed her loneliness during their courtship, but she realized that it was not the relationship she would settle for and her loneliness returned. So, feeling lonely in relationship, not good enough for her acting coach and not able to trust her thinking for fear of making a mistake, Sophia was trapped. Fearful of being alone and worried about becoming a disappointment to her parents, she had no place to go with her conflicted feelings. She tried to repress them and do what she knew how to do: work harder. But it didn't work.

Repressed feelings are ultimately removed by our body in the form of mood conditions or physical conditions. Sophia was quite literally living out her early decision of, I'm not good enough and I'm all alone," and her body began demanding her attention by creating panic attacks.

Relationship Fallout

Sophia made a choice to stop acting school and enter a liberal arts college full-time. The termination of her relationship with her acting coach was the first relationship fallout she experienced. As she began to live with her new belief, "I'm excellent at what I do and I'm loved and supported by those around me," she was unwilling to be associated with people who were hypercritical of her, and did not maintain a connection with her acting coach.

Sophia also began to confront her mother about second-guessing her and expecting her to be perfect. Their relationship was strained for several months as her mother became accustomed to Sophia's new belief system. As she grew stronger, Sophia lovingly moved on from her high school sweetheart and opened herself up to new relationships that were more balanced.

Potholes and Self-sabotage

How did Sophia experience potholes and self-sabotage after she made a decision to change, and committed to her new belief? First, she had to guard against isolating and spending time alone, which would trigger her old beliefs. Occasionally, she would set herself up to be alone by announcing to friends that she had to study. But when they got together without her, Sophia felt left out and alone, and at times experienced profound anxiety. This was always a lesson to her not to isolate, but to keep herself socially connected as she began to trust that she was good enough, all by herself, and she wasn't all alone.

Second, Sophia tended to sabotage herself by keeping herself overloaded and fatigued. She was unable to say no to friends and organizations wanting her time and resources. Sophia often became ill with allergies or colds from a compromised immune system because she kept her schedule overloaded trying to, "do enough, to be enough." Like her perfectionistic mother, Sophia second-guessed her decisions and choices, making everything unnecessarily energy-draining.

The Plan for Success

Sophia continued therapy and convinced her mother to enter therapy with her to repair their relationship. She had me make an audio CD reinforcing her affirmations and new beliefs, which she listened to twice daily for more than a year. She bought a beautiful doll that reminded her of herself as a child, and had regular role play conversations with it to remind her child self that she was good enough and could relax. She put photos of herself as a child in frames where she could see them and reassure them every day. Sophia was as diligent about reinforcing her new beliefs as she had been about everything else in her life, and she was successful.

How did Sophia structure her life to succeed? She had already developed a core group of very close friends and she learned to trust their commitment to her, whether she was physically with them or not. She lived by her new decision, completed college, went to graduate school, and married an intelligent man who adored her and is also her peer. Sophia is happily on her way to the rest of her life, free of panic attacks, and feeling supported and good about herself.

TINA AND DREW

Core beliefs: Tina's Belief: "No matter how much I give, I'm not enough."

Drew's Belief: "I'm not loved, I'm not wanted."

Tina was a lovely mother of three, who was feeling inadequate and unsure of her self-worth when she first sought help. She had been employed as a human relations executive before having children, but had decided, along with her husband, that being a stay-at-home mom for the first few years of their children's lives was more important than their dual income. Tina took on a few part-time professional projects, but primarily spent her energy taking care of their home and family.

Drew, also tall and slightly built, was a successful marketing executive moving up the corporate ladder in his company. He did not express any particular dissatisfaction with Tina except that he felt she was moody and not easily satisfied. He was surprised at the level of her unhappiness and anxious to try to improve their situation.

Family History

Tina had been raised by an overly critical mother and a passive father. No matter what her successes were in school or social events, her mother indicated that she should have done better, or could have done more. Her father remained quiet about the issues which, for a child, constitutes agreement by omission. Tina remembers trying hard to please her mother, but nothing ever seemed to be enough. As a young child, Tina began developing conditioned chemistry that formed a core belief, "I'm not enough. No matter what I do or how much I give, I am not enough."

Drew was raised in an alcoholic family system and didn't feel emotionally connected to his mother or his father. His father was an alcoholic and his mother was gone a lot. He often found himself spending time at home alone. He had clear memories of meeting his parents at the door, trying to get their attention, trying to get them to play with him, trying to get them to connect with him. It didn't work. When he couldn't connect as a child, he developed conditioned chemistry that caused him to decide, "I'm not loved, I'm not wanted and I'm all alone."

Presenting Symptoms

Drew and Tina came to me hoping to repair their marriage after she'd had an affair, breaching their marital trust. She had become seriously enamored with someone else and was questioning whether she could get her needs for emotional intimacy met within her marriage with Drew. She said that no matter how much she tried to show her love for Drew, it never seemed to be enough for him.

Tina felt like his love for her didn't have the depth she was looking for in a marriage. She wasn't sure if Drew was capable of intimate emotional connection, or if she was simply inadequate as a wife and mother. Tina was deeply afraid that she was not good enough as a wife and was so upset, she had seen her doctor for an antidepressant. Drew had implied as much to her, saying, "I never felt you loved me as much as I loved you." Drew was feeling rejected, unloved and scared. Ironically and sadly, Tina felt the same way. They argued on a regular basis and were not finding any resolution so they kept having the same arguments over and over. Neither of them wanted to be a divorce statistic, but neither wanted to continue in the unhappy situation they were living. Both of them loved their children and didn't want to split up their family.

Drew's mother had an affair when Drew was in his early teens, and eventually left his father. Drew, blaming his mother for the breakup and feeling sorry for his father, went to live with his alcoholic dad and assumed the responsibility of caring for him. Drew didn't see his mother for a number of years and his father, like all addicts, was more involved with his addiction than his son.

What children do when they cannot connect emotionally with their parents is shut down their need for intimate emotional connection and, therefore, do not develop the neural pathways that allow them to connect deeply with anyone. Consequently, since Drew was never able to feel loved and valued by either parent, he didn't develop the neurochemistry to allow him to intimately, emotionally connect with his wife.

Now, as adults, the conditioned chemistry that attracted them to each other faded as their negative core beliefs became operational in the marriage. Tina's belief that no matter how much she gave, it wouldn't be enough, caused her to marry someone with the belief that he is not loved and not wanted. No matter how much Tina tries to show her love, Drew isn't able to be sustained by it, which proves to Tina that she isn't enough. She can't "do enough or be enough" to reach Drew.

Out of frustration and loneliness, Tina reached out to another man who made her feel special, made her feel she was "enough." When Drew became aware of the breach in the relationship, his conditioned chemistry was triggered and his old belief of, "I'm not loved or wanted" caused him to feel the terrible pain once again of being ignored or rejected by his closest loved one. Tina, unwittingly, of course, had proven Drew's belief to him by becoming involved with another man.

Therapy Process

Over a period of many months, I worked with Drew and Tina, helping them change their negative core beliefs and helping them understand how those beliefs had been sabotaging their marriage. The pain Drew experienced because of Tina's affair generated anger in him that was hard for Tina to tolerate, and they ended up separating a couple of times. But Drew kept working on opening up his feelings and connecting with Tina in an intimate way. In kind, Tina continued releasing the belief that she had to be more than enough in order to be acceptable to him.

There was a period when I wondered if their marriage would make it; they actually bought a second house in preparation for divorce. But I continued to support the idea of their remaining married to each other. I could see the pain they had caused each other, but I could also see the love between them. I explained to them that, until they had successfully removed the impact of their negative core beliefs from their marriage, they would not know whether it could succeed. Furthermore, I explained that a second marriage would experience the same kind of dynamic and face the same type of resolution. Fortunately, both of them kept doing the work of getting their negative beliefs out of their relationship and gradually were able to regain their connection and save their marriage.

Relationship Fallout

Tina's relationship with her former lover came to an end, of course, and she had to give up some relationships with people who were in close contact with him. But she decided that this was a small price to pay as compared to breaking up her family. She experienced some fallout with her mother as she began to stop her mother from criticizing her, but they were able to repair their relationship over time. Drew experienced some relationship fallout with his father and mother for a while until he could reconcile the reasons for their behavior and see that they, too, were the product of their environments. Drew also chose to limit the time he spent with his single drinking buddies because, like his father, he had begun to drink too much at times.

Potholes and Self-Sabotage

At the beginning of the therapy process, when Tina was unsure about whether she could get her emotional intimacy needs met with Drew, she did sabotage the therapy process by seeing her former lover again, which caused further damage in her relationship with Drew. Drew sabotaged the repair process by drinking too much and becoming belligerent at times to Tina, and by being distant and uncommunicative. However, both of them could see the old patterns clearly and worked very hard to make the changes they needed to make.

The Plan for Success

They continued therapy and they did affirmations daily to reinforce their new beliefs ... Drew put his affirmations all over his car and office. Tina made an audio CD that she listened to first thing in the morning upon awakening and made it the last thing she did in the evening, just before going to sleep. She also wrote poetry containing all her new affirmations and placed it throughout her home and car.

Tina and Drew developed a plan whereby they would have signals for each other, known only to them, to be used when either of them spotted old patterns in the other. They made a schedule for having special time together without the children so that each of them could feed each other's need for emotional intimacy. Tina recommended, and Drew agreed, that they give each other a night off from parental responsibilities at least every other week so that they could do something to pursue their own interests. And they decided that they might actually move to a new city where they could find a broader variety of social activities.

LILLIAN AND PAUL

Lillian's Core Beliefs: "I'm not important, I don't matter, I'm all alone."
Paul's Core Beliefs: "I can't be me, I'm bad and all alone."

Lillian

Lillian was an attractive 35-year-old woman with an interesting mix of multi-faceted traits. A mother of one nine-year-old son, she was also vice-president of a local company and reported that she worked all the time. Lillian had a wonderful laugh and could be lighthearted and positive. Her fortitude was unshakable most of the time, although, on rare occasions, she and her husband, Paul, could get into marathon fights where her stress level could get to her and she could become volatile. She reminded me of an iron butterfly. She could be light, euphoric and fun-loving, but in a flash, when Paul discounted her in some way, she could either wilt and cry or morph into an iron maiden and put him on the defensive. Raised in a world where the men in her life didn't sufficiently respect women, she had developed a coping mechanism of producing an iron shield to protect herself.

Family History

The oldest of four children — three daughters and one son — Lillian was raised in a middle-class Midwestern family. Her father was a self-made successful businessman who worked all the time; mother and children worked with him in their family business.

Lillian's parents divorced when she was young and both remarried partners with younger children. Lillian lived in a blended family environment with both parents working outside the home and was kept busy taking care of younger children. She remembered that she was expected to be self-sufficient.

Lillian's father clearly favored his only son and Lillian remembers feeling left out and lonely much of her young life. She was developing conditioned chemistry and core beliefs of, "I'm not important, I don't matter, I'm all alone."

Paul

Paul was a tall, handsome man with a great laugh. At 38, he was outgoing and gregarious, and at the top of his game professionally; he worked in marketing for a large corporation. Paul was a committed Christian, working hard to be a man of high morals, faithful to his responsibility to his wife and son, and his career.

Paul had a mild to moderate bipolar mood condition, but he chose not to use medication because he didn't like its interference with his creative productivity. People with bipolar can be difficult to live with, even when they are on medication. So his moodiness and overly emotional — sometimes over the top — behavior was exasperating and painful for Lillian when she was trying to solve an issue with him.

Family History

The youngest of four children and four years younger than his next oldest sibling, Paul had grown up in an upper-middle-class family in the Southwest. His father was a professional and his mother was a stay-at-home mom.

Paul's parents had high expectations of their children and their clear attribution to them was to "be nice and don't cause any trouble." Over the years, Paul had interpreted this message as, "I can't be me." His mood condition began to develop and he had difficulty with his behavior for several years.

At first, not understanding what he was experiencing, out of frustration, his parents unintentionally conveyed a message that he was bad and, over the years, Paul developed conditioned chemistry that said, "I'm bad." He remembered spending a lot of time alone as a child. He told me, "By the time I came along, my parents were tired so I kind of raised myself." That childhood experience started the formation of Paul's core belief, "I'm all alone."

Presenting Symptoms

When Lillian and Paul came to see me they seriously doubted whether their marriage could survive, reporting that, "We can't resolve our arguments." They had been married 10 years and had one son. They told me that they were losing their friendship and had already lost their emotional intimacy. Paul reported and Lillian confirmed, that she had no interest in lovemaking.

What they described as the most intolerable situation, though, was that they fought — sometimes daily — and lived in what both of them considered to be a world of unpredictable upheaval. The hurt and anger I sensed in both of them were operating at an intense level. Their marriage was definitely in peril. However, it was clear to me that they still loved each other and neither of them wanted a divorce. I was hopeful. When I have that situation where both partners want to save the marriage and they still love each other, my success rate is over 95 percent in helping to save the marriage.

Therapy Process

I began, as I always do with my couples, by asking them to identify why they chose each other in the first place. Next, I asked them, "Each of you, one at a time, without interrupting the other, tell me what is right and what is wrong with your marriage." Paul went first. He felt that Lillian's job, which she worked on at home "all the time," was the main intruder in their life and the main reason she had lost her energy for intimate relations with him. He said, "She expects too much of me and gives more of herself to her job than to me." He also said that Lillian was too needy and should develop interests of her own so that she wouldn't feel so left out when he did things without her. Furthermore, he said, "If I disagree with her, she can shut me out and be very difficult and critical of me." Lillian, unwittingly, was triggering Paul's core beliefs of, "I'm bad, I can't be me and I'm all alone."

Next, Lillian explained what bothered her about being married to Paul. She said that her most painful issue was that he was overly engrossed in his own activities and didn't spend enough personal time with her: "We have no special time together. Furthermore, it is exhausting trying to communicate with him because he moves from one position to another, overstates the facts sometimes, and I'm never sure how he's going to react to things I need to talk with him about." Additionally, she said, "Paul doesn't listen to me before interrupting me. He treats me as if I'm not important, as if what I have to say isn't important." Paul, out of his awareness, of course, was triggering Lillian's core beliefs of, "I'm not important, I don't matter, and I'm all alone."

Over a period of two years, I helped Lillian and Paul identify and change their negative core beliefs, and helped them understand how those beliefs had been sabotaging their marriage. Once they had made new decisions and practiced their new supporting affirmations every day for a period of several months, they became much better at solving their conflict, their positive energy helped their sexual relationship and the marriage became satisfying and peaceful.

Relationship Fallout

Lillian became more attentive to her personal needs, and did not allow her career to use so much of her time, particularly at home. There was some relationship fallout with people at work, but nothing serious. Paul had some relationship fallout with a few of the social contacts he had spent so much time with each week, but he committed himself to finding the special time with Lillian that she needed, and made it a priority.

Potholes and Self-sabotage

Lillian had to be very careful not to fall back into the old routine of taking work home every day. She also had to practice her affirmations daily to remind herself of her value and importance, as she could easily slip into her aloneness and just bury herself in work.

Paul had to practice his commitment to stay connected with Lillian since he had not developed the neurochemistry to stay connected, as a child.

Plan for Success

Lillian and Paul listened to and read their new decisions and new affirmations every day for 90 days without fail. They developed self-soothing skills that helped them take time-outs from arguing when necessary. They developed physical "high signs" to alert each other when one was engaging in the old behavior, and this was very helpful in keeping them focused on their new decisions. They made a monthly date and scheduled a couple of short vacations, just for the two of them, and faithfully followed that plan. In short, Lillian and Paul did everything that was recommended to help them change their situation and they succeeded.

Read a preivew of the upcoming memoir
by Mae Chinn Songer

My Story: Growing Up With Trouble

My life, like many of yours, has been a juxtaposition of good and bad, productive and unproductive. In my upcoming memoir stories about my childhood will detail some of the events that happened in the earlier years of my life and exemplify both the good and bad experiences that acted as my foundation. These memories chronicle a sometimes perilous, but always remarkable, story of one girl's journey; a journey that was predicated on a lack of protection and support in the formative years.

The specifics of this story will hopefully provide you with insights about the emotional and physical foundations related to personality development. From the memoir's descriptions it is easy to see how I formed certain beliefs about life, about relationships, and how those core beliefs guided my life as I grew older. We each have our own unique story and everyone has challenges in his or her life. The level of deprivation that I experienced as a child was more severe than most, but many aspects of my story will resonate with aspects of your own.

Paris, France 2007

My husband Chad had been hit by a truck and was lying in the middle of the street. We were touring Paris, and had walked up the legendary Champs-Elysees to the Arch de Triumph, then decided to cross the street for the return trip to our hotel. Ahead of me Chad stepped into the intersection and was sideswiped by a white delivery truck. I watched helplessly as the side view mirror flew from the vehicle and my husband fell to the ground. Horrible images of hospitals, doctors, police…and me with my limited French trying to communicate, flashed through my mind. Bruised but not seriously injured, Chad reassured the anxious driver that he was fine as I hailed a taxi and we returned to our hotel.

Later that afternoon as Chad napped; I stood looking out of our 17th floor window. I felt such gratitude for Chad's safety and such awe for our surroundings. All the incredible architecture in the buildings across the street, the lush baskets of flowers hanging from each streetlight far below, sculptures gracing the buildings and avenues, and the artistic mélange of color enveloping awnings, doorways, windows and buildings. Our lifestyle had allowed us to travel all over the world, but as legend avows, the loveliness of Paris is incomparable.

Chad was getting up…someone had knocked. A French waiter was delivering fresh towels, chocolates, and water. I watched as my tall, handsome, husband, Judge Hugo "Chad" Songer, tipped the waiter and placed the linens on heated towel racks in the bathroom. As he moved about the room, I glanced in the antique mirror beside me, my reflection surreal. I looked at myself and thought "Lillian Mae, this is a long, long way from Prentiss, Kentucky."

Prentiss, Kentucky 1959

My life had not always been surrounded by such opulence and my thoughts wandered to an earlier time, a time when I too had almost been hit by a truck. It was 1959, in the coal mining country of southeastern Kentucky and I was running away from home. My father had beaten me and choked me until I was unconscious that day, and when I awoke, I found my mother throwing cold water in my face and my little brothers and sisters huddled in the corner, traumatized from the violence they had just witnessed. I knew that staying there was no longer an option. I left and didn't look back. I was 13, barefoot, and on a gravel road leading to an uncertain future. Hearing a motor, I jumped across the ditch into tall weeds and looked over my shoulder, fearful that it might be Dad. Instead, it was a coal truck headed for the railroad cars at Beaver Dam. I ran into the middle of the road and stood, arms outstretched. The startled truck driver had only three choices; to hit me, to hit the ditch or to stop. He swerved to a stop just missing me.

*****

This memory is always with me. It rests in my subconscious as a measurable dividing point between the dangerous life I lived as a young child and the life I managed to create as an adult. Growing up in a poor rural Kentucky family with 15 children, I dreamed of a better life. My childhood was a study in deprivation without adequate food or shelter, and constant violence. Although story telling is a different approach to disseminating information I think this story is an excellent exemplar of core belief development and the success that happens when you work to change the unhealthy ones. I have utilized parts of my life throughout this book on The Chemistry Tattoo, and believe a more complete rendition will reach additional readers. This memoir will allow you to experience the process of core belief development through narrative, rather than assimilating direct content. People learn in different ways and storytelling reaches the subconscious directly with vivid imagery, creating understandings with far less conscious effort. It is my hope that by telling my truth in the form of a narrative, it will put you in touch with your truth as well ...

CPSIA information can be obtained at www.ICGtesting.com
Printed in the USA
LVOW10s0516150813

347644LV00002B/4/P

9 781938 388323